CABOT AND BRISTOL'S AGE OF DISCOVERY

The Bristol Discovery Voyages 1480 -1508

Evan T. Jones and Margaret M. Condon

University of BRISTOL

Acknowledgements

We thank Gretchen Bauta, a private Canadian benefactor, for her generous support of the University of Bristol's Cabot Project (2011-2016). She made this book possible and we dedicate it to her. We also thank Vicky Coules (Burning Gold Productions) for helping to get the Project off the ground in 2007-8 and both the University of Bristol, Arts Faculty Research Director's Fund (2009) and the British Academy (2010) for providing further seed-corn funding. Lisa Shanley assisted us more than she will ever know in opening a window for our work in Italy, while Professor Francesco Guidi Bruscoli (University of Florence) deserves particular thanks in relation to this book for his recent work in Italian archives.

For their comments on earlier drafts of this book, we thank Royston Griffey, Rowan Mackenzie and Tony Dickens, at the *Matthew* of Bristol; Peter Pope, Bill Gilbert and Susan Snelgrove, in Newfoundland; Frank Deane, Emma Whittaker and Vicky Coules in Bristol; and Ken and Shirley Jones in Wales.

CONTENTS

Plate 1 | Ernest Board, 'Departure of John Cabot on his Voyage of 1497' (*Bristol Museum & Art Gallery*)

INTRODUCTION

Europe's discovery of the Americas in the 1490s was one of the most important events in the history of the world. New crops, animals and foodstuffs transferred across continents. Horses, pigs and wheat transformed the economies and societies of the Americas, while potatoes, maize and cassava did the same for Europe, Asia and Africa. Meanwhile, the Old World diseases inadvertently introduced to America decimated the indigenous population, allowing the rapid conquest and colonisation of Central and South America by the Spanish and Portuguese. Once there, they founded plantations and silver mines that made them rich, establishing forms of commercial exploitation that others, such as the English, would copy in North America during the seventeenth century.

Ask people today about the voyages of the late-fifteenth century and many will recall that 'In fourteen hundred and ninety two, Columbus sailed the ocean blue'.[1] Yet Christopher Columbus never ventured beyond the Caribbean. His early expeditions explored the Bahamas, Hispaniola and Cuba, and when he reached the mainland in 1498, his landing place was the coast of modern-day Venezuela, in South America. Neither he, nor any of the other explorers from Spain, visited North America before 1513.[2]

Although the Spanish did not explore to the north in the decades after 1492, they knew North America existed and even marked it on their maps. In 1500, a Spanish cartographer and explorer, Juan de la Cosa, created a world map that included the northern continent and the identity of those who had been there. The map marks a long section of coast with five English flags and the note that this was 'the sea discovered by the English'. Those explorers were the men who sailed from Bristol under the flag of Henry VII, King of England. The most famous of them was the navigator John Cabot, known in his native Venice as Zuan Chabotto. His 1497 voyage in the *Matthew* of Bristol resulted in Europe's discovery, or rediscovery, of North America. Yet his expedition was not the first exploration voyage launched from Bristol and it was not the last. Between 1480 and 1508 Bristol sent a series of expeditions into the Atlantic to search for new lands and trade routes. This book is the story of those endeavours: a tale that has Cabot at its heart, but which began decades earlier. That is why we need to start, not with Cabot, but with Bristol and the world from which the voyages sprang.

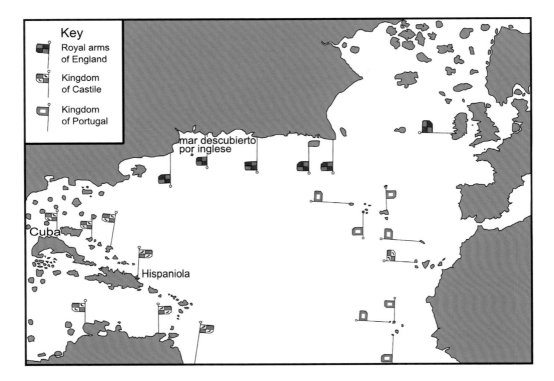

Fig 1 | 1500 AD: The North Atlantic in Juan de la Cosa's Map with English flags marking the coast 'discovered by the English' in North America. The Castilian flags record the Caribbean islands and the north coast of South America explored by the Spanish. Portuguese and Spanish flags on the Atlantic islands off Africa mark the recently-established colonies in the Azores, the Canaries and the Cape Verde Islands

1 BRISTOL IN THE AGE OF DISCOVERY

Fifteenth-century Bristol was England's leading provincial centre and the second port of the realm. By modern standards it was small, with a population of just eight thousand. Yet in a pre-industrial country of two million people, this was enough to make Bristol the regional hub for Somerset, Gloucestershire, South Wales and much of the West Midlands. The town itself was just a mile across: a visitor entering from the east on the London road could walk to the western shipyards in half-an-hour. In the process they would pass the Norman castle, the High Cross, the town's fine churches and the tall timber-framed houses of the port's great merchants. But what often impressed visitors most were the ships, glimpsed first down side alleys leading off the

Plate 2 | Bristol's High Cross and city gates as depicted in its late-fifteenth century town chronicle *(Bristol Record Office, MS 04720)*

main commercial streets to Bristol's quays. These great merchantmen were the pride of the port and carried the maritime trade on which Bristol's economy was based.

Although all towns and cities depended to some extent on commerce, Bristol was more committed to overseas trade than anywhere else in England – the capital included. In part this was because while London, the richest city in the realm, was the centre for government, law and administration, Bristol had little to distract it from foreign trade. The port was distinctive for the extent to which local men dominated commerce and shipping. In England's other major ports, foreign merchants and ships were responsible for much of the long-distance trade. In Bristol it was conducted by native merchants, mariners and ships. That gave the port the skills and equipment needed to search out new lands.

Bristol was well placed to conduct trade between the western half of the country and the ports of Atlantic Europe. In principle its overseas commerce could include Scotland, Ireland, France, Spain and Portugal. In practice, economics and politics had a big impact on Bristol's trade profile. Economics was important because merchants only visited foreign ports if they could sell their goods for a profit, or buy wares they could sell back home. Politics mattered because, even if trade with a particular port *might* be profitable, merchants only went to places when it was safe to do so. If there was a risk that their ships and goods might be seized in a foreign port, they were unlikely to go there. That limited England's trade with France, because the two countries were at war for much of the period, as part of the long conflict known today as the 'Hundred Years War' (1337-1453). And since Scotland and the Spanish Kingdom of Castile backed France in this dispute, doing business with them was also difficult.[2]

Although Bristol merchants traded with many places at the start of the fifteenth century, the bulk of their commerce was with southern Ireland and Gascony in western France. Both were subject to the English crown, which meant English merchants were well treated. Both trades were lucrative in their own ways. From the Anglo-Irish

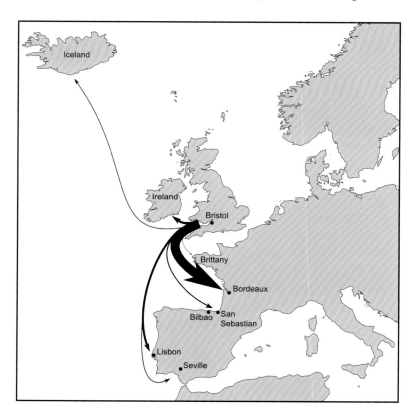

Fig 2 | Bristol's main trading partners during the first half of the fifteenth century

ports of southern Ireland, such as Waterford and Cork, came cured herring, hake, salmon and animal skins. In Bordeaux, the merchants bought wine, which accounted for almost half of Bristol's imports. Exports consisted mostly of manufactured goods, in particular the fine woollen broadcloth for which England was known across Europe.[3]

Whilst the bulk of Bristol's overseas trade was with Ireland and Bordeaux, two of Bristol's lesser trading partners are more interesting for the history of discovery: Portugal and Iceland. Portugal had been an ally of England since 1386. So Bristol merchants could sail there knowing that their ships and goods would be safe on arrival. In Lisbon, Bristol's merchants exchanged cloth for wine, olive oil and dried fruits. Although the Portuguese trade was much smaller than that to Bordeaux, at least during the first half of the fifteenth century, it employed Bristol's greatest ships, which could be in excess of 400 tons burden. These were floating fortresses, heavily armed to resist pirates from France, North Africa or Spain.

The passage to Lisbon took about three weeks: down past Cornwall, across the Bay of Biscay, and then southwards along the Portuguese coast. Once they arrived, the merchants typically spent two or three months in port, selling their cloth and using the proceeds to buy a return cargo.[4] The Lisbon run gave Bristol's merchants, ship-owners and mariners, experience of long voyages. It also gave them a 'quay-side' seat to one of the most important developments in maritime history. This was the start of the Age of Discovery, when European sailors left the familiar shores around Europe to venture across the oceans of the world in search of new lands and trade routes.

With its long Atlantic coast, Portugal was no stranger to the sea. But, at the start of the fifteenth century, nobody guessed that within a hundred years this small country would have established the most extensive seaborne empire in history – stretching from the North Atlantic to the China Sea. This owed much to the dreams of the Portuguese prince, Henry 'the navigator' (1394-1460), who began to sponsor expeditions down the African coast from c.1420 in the hope of establishing a maritime trade with the tropical kingdoms that lay beyond the Sahara. This would cut out the need to get such goods from Arab traders, who had long carried these wares across the desert by camel. Over the next seventy years, the Portuguese charted the whole west coast of Africa, as far as the Cape of Good

Hope. They also established direct trade for gold, ivory and slaves, with the sub-Saharan kingdoms, from colonies established at places such as Arguin (1445) and Elmina (1482). At the same time, the Portuguese discovered and colonised many Atlantic islands. Some

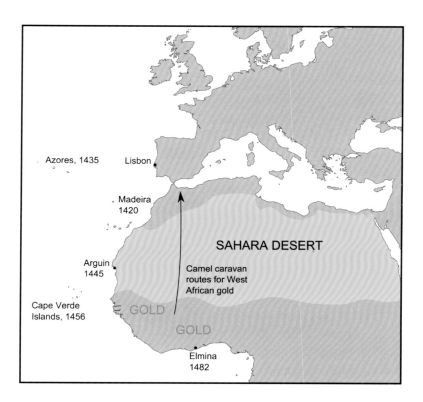

Fig 3 | Map of Portuguese exploration and discovery, c.1420-c.1482

Plate 5 | Chart of the West African coast depicting the names given to coastal features by Portuguese explorers and the fortress of São Jorge da Mina, a centre for the trade in gold and slaves: detail from Cantino world map, 1502 (*Biblioteca Estense, Modena*)

of these, such as the Cape Verde Islands (1456), had been unknown before. Others, such as Madeira (colonised from 1420), and the Azores islands (colonised from 1435), appear on earlier maps but were then effectively forgotten until the early fifteenth century. Once settled they soon became highly profitable colonies, producing sugar, sweet wine, cork and woad, the last of which was an important dye-stuff for the English and Flemish cloth industries.

Bristol merchants were well placed to witness Portugal's success. Many Bristol men lived in Lisbon, serving as agents for masters based back in England and trading from Portugal in their own right. These agents worked closely with Portuguese businessmen and some even married into Lisbon families. So they had numerous opportunities to learn what the locals were doing and to discuss the new discoveries with the English merchants that stopped-over in Lisbon on their regular voyages.[5]

Bristol's merchants were venture capitalists to the bone. Watching the success of the Portuguese sailors, they must have asked themselves: 'If they can discover lost islands and trade routes, why can't we do the same?' Competing with Portugal to the south would be difficult: they would have to travel further and it would endanger England's good relations with the country. On the other hand, for any searches to the west and north of the British Isles, Bristol had the geographic advantage. And if the Portuguese could find lost Atlantic islands, Bristol mariners also knew tales of lost lands in the Atlantic. Indeed, within a few years of the start of Portugal's voyages of discovery, Bristol's merchants were trading profitably with a 'lost' land of their own.

Just as the Portuguese were aware of the Azores before 1435, the English knew about Iceland. Trade between Scandinavia, Britain, Ireland, Iceland and Greenland had flourished during the Viking era and only died out after 1262, when Iceland became subject to Norway. The Icelanders were then ordered to trade solely through Bergen in Norway. Other nations were forbidden from sailing to the island and since the Icelanders lacked the timber needed for building large ships, they became entirely dependent on Norway. To Englishmen, Iceland thus became a 'lost' land in the fourteenth century. It was marked on sea charts and referred to in geographical works, but few, if any, Englishmen went there for several generations.[6] The fourteenth century was a bad time for Norway. Wracked by the

Black Death from 1348, it went into decline, becoming subject to Denmark in 1376 as part of the Kalmar Union. Iceland was of little interest to the Danes, to the extent that some years no ships went there at all. So when some adventurous English fishermen arrived in c.1409, they discovered a people who were keen to exchange their air-dried cod, known as 'stockfish', for the many goods the Icelanders could not produce themselves. Bristol's merchants were soon playing a major part in this business, helping to turn the 1400s into Iceland's 'English century'.

Plate 6 | Stockfish drying in the winter cold. Seen here in the Norwegian Lofoten islands, this method of drying is common to both Norway and Iceland (*Photo: Felix Lipov / Shutterstock*)

The voyage from Bristol to Iceland was a long one: 1,200 miles, west around Ireland and then northwest across the Atlantic. But it was not much further than the Lisbon run. Moreover, the Iceland voyage was complementary to the southern ones. That was because the voyages to western France and Portugal mostly took place during the autumn and winter months, when the new wine, olive oil and dried fruit became available. By contrast, the expeditions to Iceland always took place during the spring and early summer, when the weather was milder and the midnight sun made navigation less hazardous. The same great ships used in the wine trade to Lisbon and Bordeaux were used for bringing home stockfish that had been caught and 'dried in the frost' by the Icelanders the previous winter. Iceland and Portugal became the two extreme poles of

Bristol's trade, turning the port's mariners into some of the most experienced and versatile seamen of Northern Europe, navigating sea-lanes from the Arctic Circle to the Straits of Gibraltar.

The Iceland voyages prepared Bristol for further Atlantic ventures. Its mariners gained wider experience of navigating the waters of the North Atlantic, at a time when most sailors stuck to the coasts wherever possible. The 'rediscovery' of Iceland demonstrated that old stories about lost Atlantic islands were worth listening to. And from contact with the Icelanders, some of whom even settled as servants in Bristol households, Bristol merchants must have learnt that there were lands further west. The Greenland colony, which had been settled from Iceland, had only recently died out, while Bristol's merchants may also have heard older stories – of lands visited five hundred years earlier by the Icelanders' ancestors. These were the parts of North America that Leif Erikson had called Markland and Vinland, during voyages that took place around the year 1000.

2 BRISTOL AND ATLANTIC EXPLORATION: THE SEARCH FOR THE ISLAND OF BRASIL

If some lost lands proved real during the fifteenth century, not all were. Yet the search for them still proved worthwhile. Christopher Columbus is a case in point: he only discovered the Caribbean islands in 1492 because he was convinced that China and Japan lay just a few thousand miles west of Europe. But Bristol's merchants went one better. The land they sought did not exist. Yet their hunt for it led them to a new continent.

Contrary to popular myth, the mariners and geographers of fifteenth-century Europe did not believe the world was flat. Seamen and the educated knew that the world was round. So they understood that it should be possible to reach the Orient by sailing west from Europe. Centuries before the birth of Christ, Greek geographers had calculated the size of the Earth – with a fair degree of accuracy. That meant most sensible fifteenth-century scholars believed, correctly, that China must lie at least 12,000 miles west of

Plate 7 | World map from the 1482 edition of Claudius Ptolemy, Geographia[1]

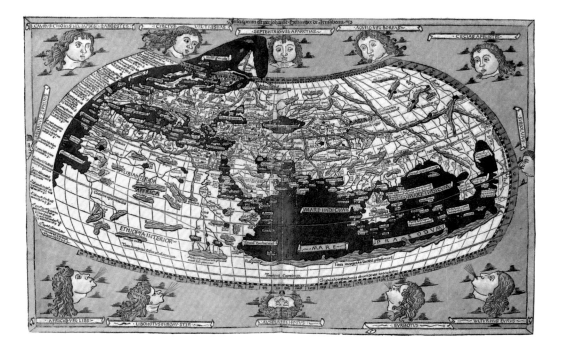

Europe, on the far side of the globe. So, the objection to Columbus' famous 'Enterprise of the Indies' was not that mariners sailing west from Europe might fall off the edge of the world; it was that a voyage of this distance would be impossible with the ships then available.

To the people of fifteenth-century Europe, the Atlantic was a dangerous ocean of unknown size. But contemporary charts show that they did not think that the Ocean was empty, at least in the waters close to Europe and Africa. In part such beliefs were rooted in reports of genuine landings or sightings. Yet the Ocean was also a place of fairy tales and monsters, populated with isles and peoples that had no basis in fact. One of these came to be the chief target for Bristol's fifteenth-century Atlantic exploration: the Island of Brasil.

Stories about Brasil, or Hy Brasil, appear to have originated in an Irish myth about an isle that lay somewhere to the west of Ireland. It was not the only mythical island the Irish imagined – they had hundreds.[2] Brasil, however, was the one that other nations believed in. By the fourteenth century both Italians and Catalans recorded it on their maps. They were the leading cartographers of the day and their charts included some genuine lost islands, such as Madeira and the Azores. So it is unsurprising that, following the success of the Portuguese in rediscovering and colonising those islands,

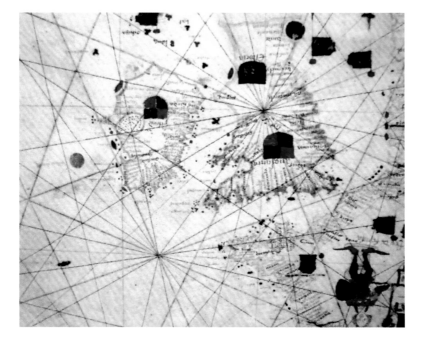

Plate 8 | The Island of Brasil depicted to the west of Ireland as a round disk: World map of the Majorcan cartographer, Jacobo Bertran, 1482 (*Archivio di Stato, Florence, CN 07 : su concessione del Ministero dei Beni e delle Attività Culturali e del Turismo*)[3]

Bristol mariners wanted to locate Brasil. After all, most of the charts suggested that the island lay no further from Ireland than the six hundred miles that separated Lisbon from Madeira.[4] Moreover, once the Iceland voyages got underway, Bristol's mariners must have realised that their regular journeys to the north, which ran west of Ireland, were taking them close to the supposed location of Brasil. This in itself may have made them interested in finding it. Yet what really made them keen to locate Brasil was not old charts. Rather it was their conviction that mariners from their port had not only landed on the island in the past, but had made good money as a result.

Sometime between 1471 and his death in 1476, the renowned Basque chronicler, Lope García de Salazar, wrote about the Isle of Brasil. His main interest was that he supposed it to be the burial place of King Arthur. But what is distinctive about his account is that he added a further detail, noting that the English claimed that:

> a vessel from Bristol found it one dawn and, not knowing that it was it, took on there much wood for firewood, which was all of brazil, took it to their owner and, recognising it, he became very rich. He and others went in search of it and they could not find it. And sometimes ships saw it but due to a storm could not reach it. And it is round and small and flat.[5]

The reference to 'brazil' in this passage is to brasilwood. This was an Asiatic timber that was imported to Europe along with the silks and spices of the Orient. Brasilwood was valued because its shavings could be used to dye cloth a deep red. This is why the ship-owner in the account supposedly became rich by selling gathered 'firewood'. It also explains why Bristol's merchants, with their eyes firmly on the 'bottom line', wanted to find the isle. It appeared that, just a few hundred miles west of their regular trading routes, lay an island that could make them fantastically wealthy.[6]

Quite how the Irish myth of the Isle of Brasil or 'Breasil' (blessed) became associated with brasilwood is unknown. It was probably just the coincidence that the two names were almost identical. In reality the island did not exist and there is nowhere in the North Atlantic that produced the dyewood. But at some point the two became associated in people's minds and they began to believe that the Isle of Brasil was a source of the wood. Indeed, once that story

was accepted, most probably assumed that the island was called 'Brasil' *because* brasilwood could be found there.

It would not have been hard for Salazar to find out about Bristol's search for the Isle of Brasil. Following the loss of Bordeaux to the French in 1453, Anglo-Spanish relations improved, leading to a ten-fold growth of trade between the two countries over the following decades.[8] No English port benefitted more than Bristol, whose merchants became regular visitors to the Basque ports of San Sebastian and Bilbao, close to where the chronicler lived. At the same time the Basques became regular suppliers of shipping services to Bristol.[9] Salazar could have heard of the search for Brasil

either by talking to Bristol's merchants directly or by speaking to the Basque shipowners, merchants and mariners who did business with them.

Salazar died in 1476, so Bristol must have commenced the search for Brasil before then. The earliest known expedition, however, took place in 1480. The voyage is mentioned in the writings of the antiquarian William Worcester, penned during a visit to Bristol.[10] Among his detailed descriptions of the town, which included him counting the length of each street in pigeon steps, Worcester noted that an 80-ton ship that was part-owned by his nephew, John Jay junior of Bristol, had been employed to search the seas to the west of Ireland for 'the Island of Brasylle'. This voyage took place from July to September 1480, the expedition being led by one 'Thloyde' (most probably John Lloyd), who Worcester says was the most knowledgeable seaman in the country. Having 'ploughed' the seas in vain for nine weeks, Lloyd gave up. Yet Bristol's merchants were not deterred; the next summer two more Bristol ships, the *Trinity* and the *George*, went on another expedition to search for the isle.

What makes the 1480 and 1481 voyages unusual is not that they were the first, or the last, English expeditions to search for Brasil. What is unusual is that there is a *record* of them. Today the Bristol expeditions are famous because they resulted in Europe's discovery, or rediscovery, of North America. But since nobody realised how important this would be, very few people wrote about the voyages at the time. So we only know about Bristol's 1480 expedition because an eccentric topographer made a note of it in his private records. In a different vein, we are only aware of the 1481 voyage because it is mentioned in an enquiry into malpractice in Bristol's customs service.

The customs duties collected on imports and exports were an important source of revenue to England's kings. But they were open to fraud. Merchants smuggled goods to avoid paying their duties, and corrupt customs officials could be bribed to help them. So, when a royal commission was set-up to investigate malpractice in Bristol, it expected to learn of deceit, corruption and other offences. In September 1481, forty-four of the city's leading merchants were summoned to give evidence to the commission, which led to several allegations being laid against Bristol's customs officers and their deputies. One of the charges examined was that Thomas Croft, one of the two collectors of customs in the port, had loaded 40 bushels of salt on the *Trinity* and the *George*, two vessels in which he owned a one-eighth part. While it was not illegal for a customs officer to be a ship-owner, officers were not allowed to engage in overseas commerce. So if Croft had been trading, it would have been an offence. Yet in this case the merchants assisting the enquiry concluded that no fraud had been committed. That was because the salt was for the 'reparacion and sustentacion of the said shippes' when they set forth 'to serch & fynde a certain Isle called the Isle of Brasile'. Moreover, they maintained, the King's customs had been paid. Soon after, Croft was pardoned by the King.[11]

Before the advent of refrigeration, fishermen needed salt to preserve their catch when operating far from home. This has led some to wonder whether the 'real' purpose of the 1481 expedition was fishing. Perhaps the salt loaded on the *Trinity* and the *George* was to preserve cod caught off the coast of North America, following a *successful* expedition the previous year?[12] The trouble with this theory is that the amount of salt involved was small relative to the size of the ships. The *Trinity* had a cargo capacity of 300 tons and of the two *different* Bristol ships named the *George*, one was of at least 50 tons burden and the other was at least 150 tons.[13] If the ships had been going on a fishing expedition, far more salt would have been needed. Indeed, based on sixteenth-century fishing practices, the *Trinity* would have needed at least sixty tons of salt to preserve a full catch. What Croft provided was 40 bushels (about one ton) for each ship.[14] This would not have lasted long if the ships had been going on a commercial fishing expedition. But it was a plausible quantity to take on a voyage of discovery in which fish might be caught as a by-product, or where game might be taken on some new land, to be preserved as salted meat for the voyage home.

Plate 13 | Packing fish into barrels to be preserved as salted fish[15]

Although the 1480 and 1481 expeditions to Brasil are the only ones for which specific information exists, they were not the last. Following John Cabot's voyage from Bristol to America in 1497, one of the Spanish ambassadors in London, Pedro de Ayala, reported that 'For the last seven years the people of Bristol have equipped two, three, four caravels to go in search of the island of brazil and the seven cities.'[16]

That the focus of Bristol's ambitions during the 1490s remained the Island of Brasil is clear from the comments of John Cabot's companions following the 1497 voyage. In a letter written to Christopher Columbus in the winter of 1497/8, the Bristol merchant, John Day, claimed that:

> It is considered certain that the cape of the said land was found and discovered in the past by the men from Bristol who found 'Brasil' as your Lordship well knows. It was called the Island of Brasil, and it is assumed and believed to be the mainland that the men from Bristol found.[17]

Day implies that Cabot had merely relocated a land found in the past by Bristol men. The link to the legendary isle and the local conviction that it was a source of brasilwood is further driven home by Day's assertion that the explorers found an artefact painted with 'brasil'. The same connection was made in a letter of December 1497, written by the Milanese ambassador in London. Commenting on the voyage the previous summer, the ambassador noted that John Cabot's Bristol companions 'believe that Brazil wood and silk are native there.'[18]

Bristol's search for Brasil has generally been told as a precursor to Cabot's more famous voyage in 1497. The 'Brasil voyages' explain why Cabot went to Bristol and why the port's merchants supported him. While this is surely true, it is far less certain that Bristol men had actually discovered America at an earlier date. The chief proponent of this theory was Professor David Beers Quinn, who suggested in 1961 that Bristol might have discovered North America at an earlier time (perhaps in 1480), but then kept this a secret so that they could exploit the fisheries off Newfoundland.[19]

Unfortunately, while it is possible that Bristol's mariners reached North America before 1497, there is no evidence that they established a fishery. And if they had, it would have been impossible to keep it secret, given that dozens of ships and hundreds of men would have been involved in the business over the years. Bristol was not a closed port and the nature of merchants and mariners was that they travelled a lot and talked a lot. They also spent a great deal of time writing to their business associates, providing updates on matters of commercial interest. It is from such letters that much of our information about Cabot's voyages comes. John Day's letter illustrates just how effective this information network could be. Cabot's 1497 expedition involved just one small ship and about twenty men, with the Venetian having good reason to keep the particulars of his voyage private. Yet, within a few months of it taking place, all the key details had been passed on to Cabot's arch-rival, Christopher Columbus. If this was true in this instance, is it really plausible that a large-scale fishery, involving dozens of ships, could have been kept secret over many years?

The great irony of Bristol's search for Brasil is that the Americas did possess a tree that produced a red dye that was very similar to that extracted from Asiatic Brasilwood. Unfortunately, the tree in question (*Caesalpinia echinata*) grew, not in the northern hemisphere, but in the Amazon rainforests of South America, where it was discovered by the Portuguese around 1500. So similar was the wood of this tree to Asiatic 'brasilwood' that the Portuguese used the same name (brasil) for the timber of their new tree. South American 'brasilwood' soon became the region's most valuable export, to the extent that the region itself became known simply as 'the land of Brasil'. This is where the modern country of 'Brazil' gets its name.

Plate 14 | South American 'Indians' collecting brasil logs for the Portuguese: detail from the Vallard Atlas *(Huntington Library, MS 29, map 11)*

By 1504 Bristol was importing New World brasil for use in the cloth dyeing industry. But it was coming via Lisbon, courtesy of Portuguese merchants.[20] If Bristol's merchants felt slightly sore about this, it would have been understandable. They had spent decades searching for the Island of Brasil and its fabled dyewood. But, in the event, it was the Portuguese who, quite by accident, discovered a dyewood with similar properties, on a new land across the Atlantic. But that land lay four thousand miles south of the seas that Bristol merchants had been exploring. The Portuguese called the dyewood 'brasil' and, as the tales had promised, the land of brasil made them rich.[21] In Bristol, it must have been salt on the wound.

Ultimately, it is unclear whether Bristol's early voyages in search of Brasil discovered anything. It is possible that Bristol mariners reached the eastern fringes of North America. Yet, if they did, they would not have found a dye-wood that could have made them wealthy. Nevertheless, the search for Brasil provided Bristol's mariners with experience of Atlantic exploration, while demonstrating to others that the port's merchants might support similar endeavours. It seems likely that this is why a Venetian navigator came to Bristol in 1495/6 with a plan of his own. It is to this man, Zuan Chabotto, known in England and America as John Cabot, we can now turn.

3 JOHN CABOT: BACKGROUND

John Cabot is the most enigmatic explorer of the Age of Discovery, so little being known about his birth, life, or even death. But recent research throws some light on where he came from and the sort of man he was.

While Cabot's origins are obscure, a 1498 letter suggests he was 'another Genoese like Columbus', which implies that his family was from the city-state of Genoa.[1] He must have moved to Venice by 1461, along with his father, Giulio, and brother, Piero, since in 1476 he became a Venetian citizen on the grounds that he had been resident there for at least fifteen years.[2] Having probably arrived while still a child, he became a fully integrated member of that proud and prosperous city-state. This is perhaps best reflected by Cabot's adoption of the Venetian form of his Christian name 'Zuan' in preference to 'Giovanni' – the latter being the common form of his name used in the rest of Italy. 'Zuan', moreover, is the form of his name that he kept in London, while its closeness to the Spanish and English forms of the name, at least when spoken, helps explain why he was known as 'Juan' during his time in Spain and 'John' in England.

Plate 15 | Signature of John Cabot [Zuan Chabotto] *(Archivio di Stato, Venice, Notarile Testamenti 735, fo 245 bis)*

The earliest record of Cabot, or 'Zuan Chabotto' as his signature has it, comes from 1470, when he was admitted to the confraternity of St John the Evangelist.[3] Confraternities were religious societies, run by laymen, that provided mutual support for members and organised festivals associated with their patron saint. The brotherhood Cabot joined was one of the most prestigious in Venice, which suggests that he was already a respected member of the community. The register that records his admission to the confraternity describes him as a 'pellizer': a merchant dealing in animal skins. But once he became a full citizen in 1476, he would have been allowed to take part in Venice's lucrative trade with the Eastern Mediterranean, on which much of the city's wealth was based.

Plate 16 | House in Venice said to have been the home of John Cabot. *(Photo: Didier Descouens)*[4]

By 1483 Cabot was visiting lands held by the 'Sultan of Egypt' and he later claimed that he had visited Mecca, albeit that would have been a dangerous enterprise for a Christian.[5] More certainly, his trade with the Mamluk Sultanate would have given him as good an understanding of the Orient and its exotic produce, such as silk and spices, as any European possessed in his day. That was because these goods were typically bought by Arab traders in India, or even in the lands around the China Sea, before being carried through the Middle East. Knowledge gleaned during Cabot's dealings with such merchants, combined with his connections to some of the leading shipbuilders and cartographers of Venice, probably gave him the confidence to develop his exploration plans.[6]

That Cabot became a famous explorer, rather than a successful but obscure Venetian merchant, was the result of a personal disaster.

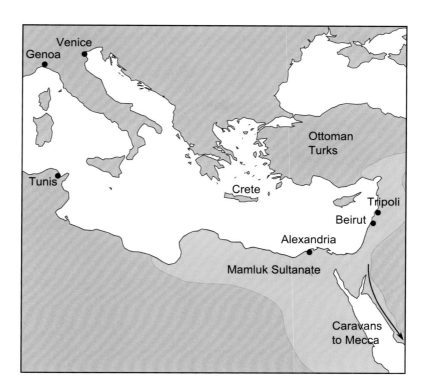

Fig. 4 | John Cabot's activities in the Eastern Mediterranean

Letters 'of justice' sent out by the Venetian government on 5 November 1488 indicate that Zuan Caboto had fled Venice as an insolvent debtor, owing money to some of the most prominent men of the city.[7] It seems that some deal or contract he had undertaken had gone sour. Rather than face imprisonment for debt in Venice, as well as the confiscation of all his property, Cabot escaped with his wife, Mattea, and their three sons: Ludovico, Sebastian and Sancio.

From 1490 to 1493 'Juan Caboto de Montecalunya', as he became known, lived in the Spanish port of Valencia, one of the greatest cities of the Kingdom of Aragon. During this period he sought employment as a civil engineer, at one point making proposals to King Ferdinand to improve Valencia's harbour facilities.[8] In so doing, Cabot may have been drawing on his experience of house-building in Venice, where all construction requires an understanding of how to build in seawater. Although his plans were considered seriously, they were not taken up; there was good will, but no money. After that, Cabot moved to Seville, where he was contracted in September 1494 to build a stone bridge over the Guadalquivir River. This would have been the first such bridge over the waterway, which had long relied on a pontoon bridge for traffic from the east

Plate 17 | The pontoon bridge across the Guadalquivir River

bank to the west. Unfortunately, the construction of such a bridge proved impossible, either then, or for many centuries afterwards. By Christmas Eve 1494 it was clear that the project was not going well and the City Council ordered an investigation. Shortly after, Cabot's contract was terminated, leaving him unemployed. At that point he had been resident in the city for at least five months.[9]

While Cabot did not succeed as a civil engineer, his life in Seville, with contacts among the city's elite, must have connected him

Plate 18 | Ferdinand II of Aragon, the patron of Cabot the engineer, and Isabella of Castile, the patron of Columbus the explorer, from a late sixteenth century portrait relief, University of Salamanca *(Photo: Procy/ Shutterstock)*

to those involved in the Spanish voyages of discovery led by Christopher Columbus. From the outset, Seville (including its outport of Cadiz) was the centre for Spain's colonisation and exploitation of the Americas. It was the city from which Columbus launched his second voyage to the New World in September 1493, with a fleet of seventeen ships and 1,200 men. So, although Columbus himself returned from this second voyage only in 1496, Cabot was perfectly placed to receive the latest news from the colonists, explorers and supply ships returning from the Caribbean.[10]

Columbus' expedition of 1492-3, along with reports coming back of his second voyage, proved that there were large unknown islands to the west. These Columbus believed to be part of the Indies and he thought that China lay just a few hundred miles beyond. Yet, by the end of 1494, there was ample evidence that these strange new lands had little to do with the Orient described by Marco Polo: no silks or oriental spices had been brought back and no great civilisation had been encountered.

Like Columbus, Cabot thought that China and Japan could be reached by sailing west, but he believed that there was a better way to get there. Columbus' expeditions had taken him into the tropics; if Cabot followed a more northerly route, the distance to China would be shorter. Following such a route he might slip past the Spanish expeditions and reach the Orient before Columbus.

Pedro de Ayala, the Spanish Ambassador in London, reported in 1498 that Cabot had sought support for his plans in Seville and Lisbon before he came to England.[11] If this is correct, it is unlikely that it was official support Cabot looked for. By the end of 1493 the Spanish monarchs had thoroughly committed themselves to Columbus. They granted him monopoly rights to explore to the west and publically endorsed his claims that the lands discovered the previous year were part of the Indies. The King of Portugal, meanwhile, had little reason to be interested in Cabot's ideas. In part this was because the Portuguese had their own plans for reaching India by sailing around Africa. More immediately, they were unlikely to back voyages across the Atlantic given that in June 1494 Portugal and Spain had signed the Treaty of Tordesillas to resolve their differences over the regions each could exploit. The treaty agreed that Spain would have monopoly rights over any land

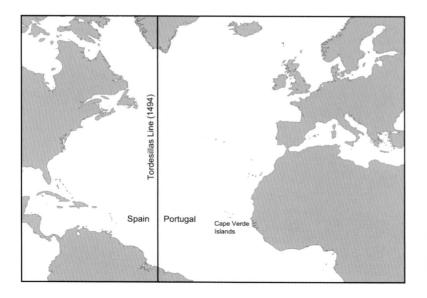

Fig 5 | Treaty of Tordesillas: Line of demarcation between Castile and Portugal

that lay more than 370 leagues (1,362 miles) west of the Cape Verde Islands, while the Portuguese would take any lands that lay east of the meridian, or line of longitude, running north and south from that point. In effect, this divided the world into two hemispheres, with Spain assuming the right to exploit the western one, while the eastern half was reserved to Portugal. For Portugal to have backed a voyage across the Atlantic by Cabot would have been in direct contravention of a treaty on which the ink had barely dried.

If Cabot sought support in Seville and Lisbon before coming to England, it seems likely that the people he talked to were the ones who ultimately backed him. These were the merchants and financiers of Bristol and Italy. By the 1490s Bristol had extensive dealings with southern Spain, which continued alongside its traditional trade with Portugal.[12] Together, the commerce to southern Iberia accounted for around forty percent of Bristol's overseas trade. The port's merchants were also exploring the North Atlantic themselves. Having witnessed the success of Spain's Italian navigator, Christopher Columbus, it is possible that Bristol merchants in Seville approached Cabot, or more likely were approached by him, to see if he might assist their search. At the same time, Cabot's connections with the Italian merchant and banking community in Lisbon and Seville could have persuaded him that he might get funding for a westward venture from the London branches of these firms.

During this period the Italians ran Europe's most complex, large-scale and long-distance commercial enterprises. While the headquarters of these firms were typically in Italy, they maintained numerous branches in Europe's principal cities.[13] Italy's venture capitalists had long had, and would long maintain, an interest in exploration and colonisation beyond Europe. Indeed, the importance of Italy's moneymen was such that the extra-European ventures launched from Iberia might best be regarded as Italian mercantile ventures undertaken under foreign flags – rather than as great 'national' endeavours. The part played by Italian explorers such as Columbus, Cabot and Vespucci in the service of foreign countries has long been celebrated. Modern research has shown that many Italian financiers supported the discovery voyages in the hope that lucrative commercial opportunities would follow.[14] But Cabot could do nothing without royal approval. Given the importance of the Italian banks to Europe's exploration voyages, Cabot's conversations with his fellow merchants may have suggested that, although it would be impossible to carry out his plans from Iberia, if he obtained support from Henry VII of England, he should get backing from some of the English branches of Italian firms. This would explain why, when Cabot left for England around the middle of 1495, he did not go to Bristol. Instead, he went to London, where the Italian colony was based.

Fig 6 | Cabot's travels following his flight from Venice

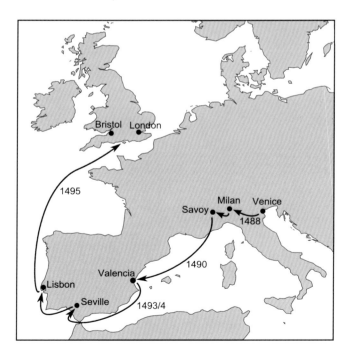

Plate 19 | John Cabot after his arrival in England. Sitting on a baulk of timber, Cabot contemplates his next move.
Stephen Joyce (1986)
(Photo: Bob Cheung / Shutterstock)

4 CABOT'S PLAN:
LONDON AND BRISTOL

On 5 March 1496, Henry VII granted 'John Cabot, citizen of Venice' the right, by 'letters patent':

> to sail to all parts, regions and coasts of the eastern, western and northern sea, under our banners, flags and ensigns…to find, discover and investigate whatsoever islands, countries, regions or provinces of heathens and infidels, in whatsoever part of the world placed, which before this time were unknown to all Christians.[1]

If Cabot succeeded, he and his heirs would enjoy the profit from any lands occupied or trade established. For his part the King would receive one fifth of all profits made from the enterprise. As with a modern patent, the grant gave the holder the sole right to exploit his 'product'. That meant the King's subjects could only sail to any lands discovered with Cabot's permission. But the grant did more than this: since Cabot's ships would be sailing under the King's colours, any attack on the explorers would be treated as an attack on the King. Foreign powers would know that, if they interfered with the expedition, England would retaliate. So while Henry VII did not pay for the venture, the legal and political guarantees were significant.

Obtaining the patent was crucial to Cabot: without it, his voyages might not have taken place. The grant, however, represented the end of a process, not the beginning of one. A poor Italian merchant could not have obtained a royal privilege like this on his own; just to get an audience with the King required influential backers. But who were these people and why did they help this bankrupt Venetian?

It used to be assumed that Cabot's supporters all came from Bristol. After all, it was on a Bristol ship, with Bristol men, that Cabot sailed. Moreover, contemporary commentators made clear that the port's merchants played a key part in the enterprise. This is apparent from a letter sent on 18 December 1497 by Raimondo

Plate 20 | The 'office copy' of the grant to John Cabot and his sons
(*TNA: C76/178 m.8*)

Plate 21 | Henry VII's great seal, which would have been attached to the actual letters patent given to John Cabot

de Raimondi de Soncino, the Milanese ambassador to England. Soncino's letter to his master, the Duke of Milan, discusses both the voyage undertaken by Cabot the previous summer and the one planned for 1498.[2] The ambassador, who had no reason for exaggerating Bristol's importance, noted that when Cabot returned four months earlier, he would not, as a 'foreigner and a poor man' have been believed at Court 'had it not been that his companions, who are practically all English and from Bristol, testified that he spoke the truth'. Soncino then went on to say of the plans for the 1498 voyage that 'the leading men in this enterprise are from Bristol, and great seamen.'

Plate 22 | Ludovico Maria Sforza, Duke of Milan. His ambassador's letters home are an important source of information concerning John Cabot. *(Victoria and Albert Museum)*[3]

Clues as to why Bristol supported Cabot can be found in the letters patent. While this was issued to the explorer, such grants could be assigned to others, in whole or part. In the same way that modern venture capitalists will buy shares in an enterprise from an entrepreneur who has a patent, Cabot could give away part of his rights to others in return for the money needed to fund his expeditions. In theory such investors could have come from anywhere. In practice, a clause in Cabot's grant made it particularly likely that Bristol's merchants and, indeed, the port's broader community, would support him. This clause was the stipulation that all ships operating under the patent should use the port of Bristol 'at which they are bound and holden only to arrive'. All future trade was to be conducted through Bristol. This made investment in the enterprise particularly attractive to the port's merchants. It would

Plate 23 | The town quays of the port of Bristol in 1673: detail from Millerd Map (*Bristol Record Office: Photo Roger Leech*)

also benefit the town more generally, since more trade would flow through it if Cabot's plans succeeded.

During the sixteenth century, Lisbon and Seville became two of the richest cities in Christendom precisely because the Portuguese and Spanish monarchs decreed that all extra-European trade should pass through these ports. The result was that the fortunes made from colonial commerce were not limited to those who were directly involved in it; many people in Seville and Lisbon became rich by providing ships, provisions and services to the trade. With Bristol being granted very similar monopoly rights in 1496, the potential rewards for the port and its inhabitants were as great as they were for Cabot.[4]

While Bristol's role in Cabot's voyages has always been clear, the significance of the Italian community in London has only recently become apparent. During the 1960s Dr Alwyn Ruddock, an historian and lecturer at the University of London, found documents that cast new light on how and why the voyages came about. Ruddock's discoveries showed that part of Cabot's funding came from Italian banks based in London. She also suggested that his chief supporter in England was Brother Giovanni Antonio de Carbonariis, an Augustinian friar from Milan. He was no ordinary friar: Carbonariis was an important ecclesiastical administrator, with responsibility for collecting the Pope's taxes in England. He was also a diplomat who served as Soncino's guide and advisor when he arrived in England as ambassador for the Duke of Milan. If Cabot had the support of such a man, it would go a long way to explaining how the would-be explorer got access to the King. That Carbonariis was involved in the later voyages is certainly known, in that he sailed on Cabot's 1498 expedition. Ruddock, however, appears to have found evidence that the friar was the explorer's chief supporter from the very start, suggesting that Carbonariis arranged Cabot's audiences with the King and, later on, secured the explorer's rewards.[5]

Plate 24 | Austin Friars, London. The friars ministered to London's Italian community, and Cabot may have lodged there.[6]

The great tragedy here is that, while Alwyn Ruddock's research was ground-breaking, she never published her findings and on her death in December 2005 she ordered the destruction of her draft book, her notes, and the photographs she had taken of her sources. Since that time the authors of this book, along with our collaborators, have sought to relocate the twenty-three new documents Ruddock said she had found during the four decades she spent investigating the Cabot voyages.[7] Our research is discussed in a number of academic articles and document transcriptions that can be accessed online. To date, not all of the documents Ruddock found have been re-discovered, which makes it impossible to verify all her claims. On the other hand, we have re-located many of her sources. These include the accounts of the Bardi, a famous Florentine banking house that had a branch in London. One of the Bardi's commercial ledgers includes a record of two payments, totalling 50 nobles (almost £17) to John Cabot in April and May 1496 to help fund his expedition to search for 'the new land'. Although their contribution would only have covered a part of Cabot's expedition costs, it confirms that he received money from the Italian merchant community in London.[8]

Plate 25 | Late fifteenth-century decoration of a beam and ceiling in the Bardi's house in Florence. It includes a frieze of nautical imagery
(Photo: Francesco Guidi Bruscoli)

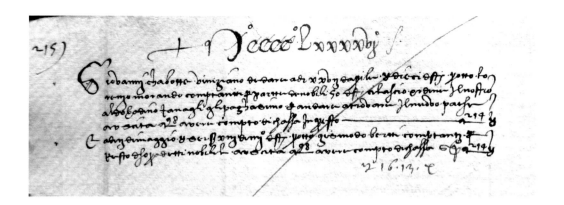

At the very least this demonstrates that the Bristol voyages were not purely a local venture. Indeed, from the perspective of his Italian backers, they might be regarded as part of their broader drive to search for new markets beyond Europe. To the Italians, Bristol's merchants and Henry VII were simply another set of partners in their search for new commercial opportunities.

Cabot's chief aim, as he described it following his 1497 voyage, was to reach China and Japan by sailing west across the Atlantic. Like Columbus, the Venetian knew that the Orient produced many luxury goods that Europeans wanted, such as silk and spices. The problem was that these goods were very expensive because of the vast distances they had to travel. Some goods spent 'a year on the road' before reaching Europe, passing through the hands of many merchants. Each of these merchants needed to pay the cost of transporting the goods, as well as any customs duties levied on the lands they passed through. And, of course, each merchant also needed to make a profit. The result was that oriental goods could cost ten times more in Europe than in their countries of origin. So, if a European merchant could sail to those countries directly, buy at the local rate and ship the goods home at low cost, he would become rich. This is precisely what Columbus hoped to do. His expeditions were based on the assumption that the world was much smaller than it actually is, and that India and China lay just a few thousand miles west of Europe. Indeed, according to his initial projections, made before he set sail, the coast of China was at least a thousand miles east of where we now know the coast of North America to be. This is why Columbus declared that the Caribbean islands he discovered in 1492 were part of the 'Indies' and that China must be nearby. Cabot clearly believed something very similar. Indeed, on his return in 1497 he suggested the lands he had discovered in North America were those of the 'Grand Khan', by which he meant the Emperor of China.[9]

While Cabot's plan was similar to that of Columbus, what distinguished it was the route he meant to follow. Columbus had sailed south to the Canaries, before heading west to the Caribbean. By contrast, having left Bristol and passed Ireland, Cabot headed north before going west. His voyage thus ran on a line that was roughly parallel to the route taken by Columbus, but more than 1,500 miles to the north. If the world had actually been much smaller, this would indeed have made a lot of sense, in that he would be arcing over the top of the world and might have reached Asia much faster. It was also a route that took advantage of the prevailing winds and ocean currents.

If Cabot's aims are clear, those of his backers are less obvious. First, it seems that his Bristol supporters hoped that his voyage would locate the Island of Brasil. They must also have bought into Cabot's hope of finding a new trade route to the Orient. Beyond this, it has sometimes been argued that Bristol was interested in sailing west because the port's merchants wanted to find new fishing grounds. This is because, when the 1497 expedition returned, Cabot's Bristol companions reported that 'the sea there is swarming with fish' and that 'they could bring so many fish that this kingdom would have no further need of Iceland, from which place there comes a very great quantity of the fish called stockfish'.[10] This fishery, which lies along the coast of Newfoundland, later became one of the world's most important cod fisheries. This does not mean, however, that the explorers had set out to find such a fishery. Indeed, the actions of Bristol men both before and after Cabot's expeditions demonstrates that they were not particularly interested in developing such a fishery themselves.

As noted earlier, when in the early fifteenth century Bristol merchants started trading to Iceland, their main purchase was stockfish – a form of freeze-dried cod that keeps for many months. Yet even at the trade's height, only a few Bristol ships sailed to Iceland each year, with the Iceland venture never accounting for more than about five percent of Bristol's overseas commerce.[11] Moreover, having reached a peak during the middle decades of the century, Bristol's trade to Iceland went into decline. Bristol's surviving customs accounts show that only one ship entered from Iceland in the accounting year 1485/6; none is reported in the customs records for 1486/7; and only one in 1492/3, which was the last known voyage from Bristol to the island.[12] By the 1480s, Bristol's 'Iceland venture' was a dying concern undertaken by only one or two ship-owning merchants.

The decline of the Iceland trade has led some historians to suggest that the English were 'forced' out of Iceland by the Hanseatic League and that this prompted Bristol to go searching for a new source of fish to the west.[13] There are a number of problems with this theory. First, it ignores the fact that, throughout the fifteenth century, most of Bristol's fish came from southern Ireland. If Bristol needed more fish, the Irish trade could have been expanded. The second problem is that the English were not 'forced out' of Iceland during this period; Hull merchants, for example, continued to trade to Iceland until the end of the century.[14] Indeed, the English fishery off Iceland actually grew in the late-fifteenth century and on into the sixteenth century. By the 1530s it was one of England's most important fisheries, with up to 130 ships sailing there annually.[15] It is just that nearly all of

Fig 7 | Bristol's trade as recorded in the 1492/3 customs accounts[17]

these vessels came from East Anglia. Bristol's merchants did not participate in the Iceland fishery because Bristol had never been much of a fishing port – the interests of its merchants were in trade, not fishing. So, it would have made no sense for them to search for a new fishery across the Atlantic that they did not need, and showed, in the event, little interest in exploiting.

That Bristol merchants stopped going to Iceland in the later fifteenth century is best explained by rising trading opportunities in Spain after 1453, as relations between England and Castile improved following the end of the Hundred Years War. This led to a dramatic increase in Bristol's commerce with Spain, which soon became much larger than its trade with Iceland had ever been. Bristol's merchants were not 'pushed' out of Iceland, they simply abandoned it in favour of more profitable opportunities in Iberia.[16] In particular, the summer trade to Iceland for fish was replaced by a higher value trade to the Basque ports of northern Spain for iron and woad.

5 1496 AND 1497 EXPEDITIONS

Once Cabot received his patent in March 1496 he was keen to sail. The only record of his voyage that summer is a letter to Christopher Columbus, written in early 1498 by the Bristol merchant, John Day:

> *Concerning the first voyage which your lordship wants to know about, what happened was that they took one ship, and he [Cabot] was unhappy with the crew and he was badly provisioned and he found the weather to be unfavourable, so he made the choice to come back.*[1]

This unsuccessful expedition seems to have been a rushed affair, undertaken too late in the year. Until Cabot secured his patent on 5 March it would have been difficult to secure funding; and even after that it took some time to get the money to pay for the voyage. The Bardi, for example, did not make their initial payment until 27 April, followed by a second instalment on 2 May. Ideally Cabot should have been at sea by then – as he was in both 1497 and 1498. Yet, since he was still collecting money in London in May 1496, it is unlikely that he could have scratched together a ship, crew and provisions before late June or July.

After his return to Bristol, Cabot had at least eight months to prepare his next venture. The interval allowed him to charter the ship of his choice and to make sure it was well provisioned. Above all, it gave him time to gather a crew who were willing to undertake a voyage of unknown length in uncharted waters.

The ship chosen for the 1497 expedition was the fifty-ton *Matthew* of Bristol. She was provisioned for an eight-month voyage. Contrary to popular belief, there is no particular reason to think the *Matthew* was specially built for Cabot; and her subsequent employment was in Bristol's ordinary trade to Ireland and France. The bare details of the ship's most famous voyage are recorded in an Elizabethan chronicle:

This year, on St. John the Baptist's Day [24 June 1497], the land of America was found by the Merchants of Bristow in a shippe of Bristowe, called the Mathew; the which said ship departed from the port of Bristowe, the second day of May, and came home again the 6th of August next following.[2]

Plate 27 | This 1951 statue by Sir Charles Wheeler stands at the entrance to Bristol's City Hall. A pensive John Cabot clutches his letters patent; an astrolabe, a portable scientific instrument used as an aid to navigation, hangs from his belt. Artistic licence has been used to depict the letters patent: in reality, they would have been little bigger than his hand (*Photo: Jamie Carstairs*)

Other accounts of the voyage were written in Cabot's lifetime, in four letters written in the months after the expedition's return.[3] None were written by Cabot, or by anyone who was directly involved in the voyage. The earliest known, written by a fellow Venetian merchant, seems to be based partly on reports of conversations with Cabot, but survives only in copy. The second letter, a dispatch to the Duke of Milan of news from England, mentions Cabot's voyage only in passing. Five months later, the diplomat Raimondo de Soncino, again writing to the Duke of Milan, combined a report of actual conversations with Cabot and his companions, with tittle-tattle about future plans.

The exception to the newsletter format of the London-based merchants and diplomats was John Day's letter to Columbus. This was sent by a Bristol merchant to a man who was interested in gleaning the exact details of where Cabot had sailed and what he had found. This was because Columbus had not achieved what he had set out to do. Although he had sailed to many islands in the Caribbean, and established a colony, he had not reached the mainland and had certainly not discovered the Orient. He still

Plate 28 |
Posthumous
portrait of
Columbus
by Sebastian
de Piombo
(*Metropolitan
Museum of Art*)

believed, however, that China lay not much further west. This made Cabot a dangerous competitor who threatened his territorial and commercial interests. If an English expedition, backed by Henry VII, reached the Orient before Columbus, it would be difficult to stop them trading there. So the Grand Admiral of the Ocean Sea needed to know where the Bristol expedition had gone.

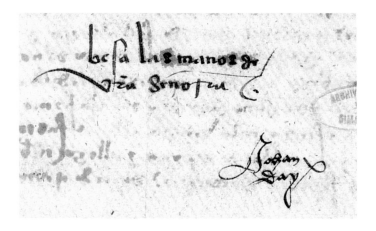

Plate 29 | 'I kiss the hands of your lordship' [signed] Johan Day (Archivo General de Simancas, Autografó 103)

According to John Day, the *Matthew* had twenty men on board. This included Cabot and two friends: one from 'Burgundy' (the Netherlands) and the other from Genoa in Italy, a 'barber' who may have served as the ship's surgeon.[4] The size of the crew was slightly larger than on a typical commercial voyage, but this was no ordinary venture.[5] If someone died, or became sick, he could not be replaced at the next port. So, it made sense to carry additional crew and to take more provisions than might be needed for a summer reconnaissance expedition. One or two merchants may also have been on board. If so, they probably included the Bristol merchant William Weston, who received a reward from the King in January 1498 and was later to lead an independent voyage of discovery from Bristol.[6]

Once the *Matthew* had passed Ireland, Day says that she headed north 'for some days' before turning west. This first passage took the explorers into waters that Bristol's mariners knew well from their voyages to Iceland and their long search for the Isle of Brasil. The difference was that Cabot carried on, sailing for thirty-five days until he sighted land. The exact location of his landfall has long been disputed: until the discovery of John Day's letter in the mid-1950s it had been placed as far south as New England or as far north

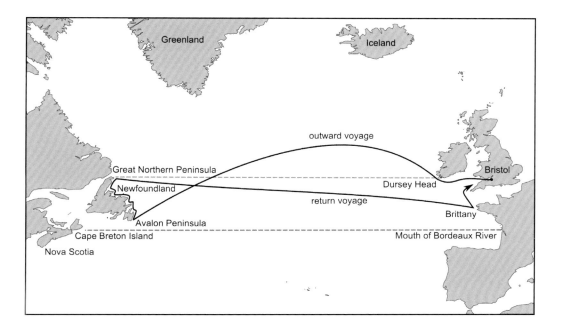

Fig 8 | Probable route of 1497 voyage

as Labrador. What makes Day's letter valuable in this respect is that he provided the latitude of two of the areas Cabot explored. This would have been a crucial point to Columbus, since it would have given him a clear idea of where the lands were, relative to those he had charted himself. The information would also have been prized because the latitudinal position of Cabot's discoveries was the one thing that the explorer could have calculated reasonably accurately using a cross-staff or astrolabe. By contrast, any assessment of how far east or west the lands lay, that is, their longitude, would have relied on the navigator's estimates of the distance travelled each day, which was difficult to determine at sea. The southernmost point Day mentions lay due west of the 'Bordeaux river' in France. By this he would have meant the mouth of the Gironde estuary in Gascony. The northernmost point lay due west of Dursey Head, in southwest Ireland. If these two points represented the latitudinal limits of the land explored, which would have been what Columbus would have been most interested in, it implies the coast investigated that year was limited entirely, or almost entirely, to Newfoundland – ranging from just below the Avalon Peninsula, on the south coast of the island, to the end of the Great Northern Peninsula. Day indicates that the expedition returned home from the northerly point mentioned, following a thirty-five day exploration of the coastline. It seems likely that the initial landfall was made fairly close to the southernmost point mentioned, in that Day says that 'it was on the way back that were found most parts of the lands that were discovered'. This suggests an initial landing on the Avalon Peninsula in Newfoundland but does not entirely rule out Bonavista, which lay about 160 miles north and which later tradition reputed as the landfall. Equally, it does not exclude Cape Breton Island, south west of Newfoundland.

All three main commentators on the voyage, including Day, indicate that the crew only disembarked once, close to where they first sighted land.[8] There, Cabot raised the banners of the Pope and the King of England, asserting legal possession of the land as an English territory, subject to the religious authority of Rome. This symbolic act of appropriation was directed at a European audience. It stated clearly that the land was 'now known to Christians' and that it belonged to the King of England. John Day says of Cabot that 'since he was there only with a few men, he did not dare to penetrate into the land any further than a crossbow's shot'. However, they did find clear evidence that the place was inhabited. Two of the accounts state that the explorers discovered the remains of a fire, a trail and various tools, one of which had been painted red with what they thought to be 'brasil' dye. It seems likely the objects found by the explorers had been left behind by Newfoundland's native Beothuk people, hunter-gatherers known for their love of

Plate 30 | A statue of John Cabot gazes across Bonavista Bay from Cape Bonavista, the place where, according to tradition, he first sighted land (*Photo: William Gilbert*)[7]

red ochre, a red earth pigment found on the island.[9] With this they painted themselves, their houses and tools. So the red 'paint' found on the tool was probably ochre.

Following their month-long exploration of the coast, the explorers made exceptionally good time on their return voyage, managing the 2,200 mile crossing of the Atlantic in just fifteen days. Reaching Bristol on 6 August, despite a navigational error on the part of his crew that took him via Brittany, Cabot barely caught his breath before riding to the manor of Woodstock, ten miles north of Oxford, to inform the King of his success. He must have been granted an immediate audience, for the King's account books record a payment to the explorer on 10 or 11 August. It is a brief note, made only to document the King's personal reward of £10 to 'hym that founde the new isle'.[10] Given that an ordinary labourer earned about £5 per year, this was not an insignificant sum. More would come later, as Cabot prepared his third voyage.

Plate 31 | The 'palace' of Woodstock in 1714[11]

Plate 32 | 'Item to hym that founde the new Isle – x li' [£10]: Henry VII's gift to Cabot
(*TNA: E101/414/6, fo. 83v*)

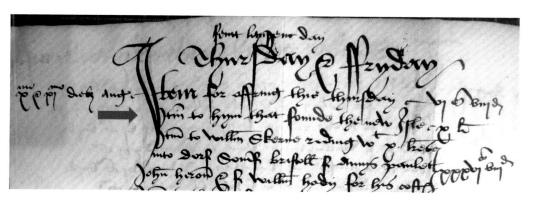

Plate 33 | Henry VII by Michael Sittow (*National Portrait Gallery*)

Although John Cabot was not 'showered with gold' on his return, some fuss was made of him and the explorer was certainly not shy about his success. On 23 August, Lorenzo Pasqualigo, a Venetian merchant in London, wrote to his brother that 'that Venetian of ours' is 'called the Great Admiral and vast honour is paid to him and he goes dressed in silk, and these English run after him like mad.'[12] The tone is slightly tongue-in-cheek, perhaps in the knowledge that, back home in Venice, Cabot's status was that of a renegade bankrupt. In England, by contrast, Cabot's admirers were comparing him to Columbus, whose official title, the 'Grand Admiral of the Ocean Sea', was now being mimicked by Cabot's friends. The Venetian would no doubt have appreciated the compliment and already had plans to live up to the flattery by leading a much larger expedition the following year. With this, he hoped to sail on to the civilised parts of the Orient, which he thought lay not much further west.

Unfortunately for Cabot, the excitement that followed his return did not last long: events intervened. Just four weeks after the explorer's return, the Yorkist pretender Perkin Warbeck landed in Cornwall to raise a rebellion against Henry VII: the second uprising that year. It was a serious threat to a King who had only come to power twelve years earlier. With an army to mobilise and a crown to preserve, it seems unlikely that the King paid much attention to Cabot over the following weeks. Indeed, he could have been entirely forgotten but for the fact that Brother Giovanni Antonio de Carbonariis, Cabot's companion on the 1498 voyage, played a role in the military emergency.

Carbonariis was at Exeter when the rebels tried to capture the city on 17 September and when Warbeck withdrew from the city, the friar seems to have followed them to Taunton. By 20 September it was clear that the uprising was failing and people started to desert. That night Warbeck fled, abandoning his rag-tag army.[13] According to a letter from the Milanese ambassador, written just a few days later, Carbonariis then 'went with all speed to Woodstock', where the King was gathering his army, 'and brought word of everything. Accordingly his Majesty dismissed all his army except 6,000 men, with whom he himself is going into Cornwall.'[14] Henry had good reason to be grateful to the friar. One beneficiary appears to have been Carbonariis' protégé, John Cabot. On 26 September the explorer had an audience with the King at Burford, while Henry

Fig 9 | Warbeck's campaign in England in September 1497

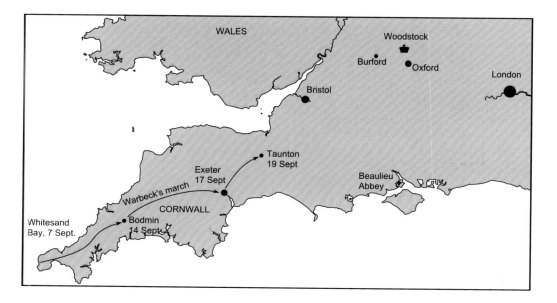

1496 AND 1497 EXPEDITIONS   47

was en-route to the West. Cabot was given another small reward, this time of £2. More importantly, it seems likely that promises were made that further gifts would follow and that there would be royal support for a new expedition: a voyage in which Carbonariis would take part.[15]

Henry VII remained in the West Country for nearly six weeks.[16] Warbeck had fled to sanctuary at Beaulieu Abbey in Hampshire, but surrendered in return for the promise of his life. On 5 October, he appeared before the King at Taunton, where he admitted publically that his claim to be the younger son of Edward IV was false, effectively ending the rebellion. The King finally returned to London in late November, at which point the normal business of government resumed. Henry now had more time for Cabot. Soon after the King's return the explorer made a presentation to the King and Council, illustrating his case with both a 'globe' and maps. Money followed: on 13 December the explorer was granted a pension, or annual salary, of £20 per year to be paid during the King's 'pleasure'.[17] This put Cabot formally into the King's service, with the pension backdated to 25 March 1497, just to make clear that Cabot had also been in the King's service when he had discovered the new lands the previous summer. Those lands had been claimed in the King's name, with a display of the King's banner, by a paid servant of the King. As far as Henry was concerned, they belonged to him.

Plate 34 | The King's devices: the Tudor colours of green and white, with dragon, greyhound and portcullis (just visible) and the royal arms (*TNA, E33/3/1*)

6 THE MYSTERY OF
THE 1498 VOYAGE

By the time Cabot was granted his pension in December 1497, he had clear plans for the following year. These are detailed in Soncino's letter of 18 December, based on his conversations with Cabot and his Bristol supporters. The explorer's intent was to return to the newly-discovered land and then:

> keep along the coast from the place at which he touched, more and more towards the east [i.e. the Orient], until he reaches an island which he calls Cipango [Japan], situated in the equinoctial region [near the equator], where he believes that all the spices of the world have their origin, as well as the jewels.[1]

To Cabot, this was all about trade. He believed the coast explored the previous summer was part of Asia, and that he could follow it west and south until he came to the civilised parts of the 'East'. There he could buy goods for a fraction of their price in Europe. When they were sold back home, he and his investors would become rich. Unlike the voyage of 1497, this was not a simple reconnaissance expedition. Cabot planned to take a small fleet of ships, confident that some would be equipped by the King. There was even talk of a colony being established, while a number of 'poor Italian friars', led by Carbonariis, would bring Christianity to the new land.

John Day's letter, written in early 1498, states that the explorers hoped to send 'ten or twelve vessels' on the next voyage. However, by 3 February, when Cabot was issued with his second letters patent by the King, his plans seem to have been scaled back. This grant did not replace Cabot's 1496 patent: its purpose was merely to assist preparations for the new voyage. In particular, it gave the explorer permission to charter up to six English ships, each of not more than 200 tons, paying only the rates that would be charged if they were in the King's service. The patent also made a general order that English officials should not hinder his plans, or subject the explorer to restrictions while he prepared his expedition.[2]

In the event Cabot sailed with five ships, departing at the beginning of May with provisions for a year. The Great Chronicle of London spells out the commercial ambitions of those involved.[3] Various trade goods, ranging from small manufactured items to bulk commodities, were dispatched on the ships. This cargo included cloth, caps and laces, sent by both London and Bristol merchants.[4] The difficulty for the investors was that, while they knew what they wanted to buy in the Orient, they had no idea what the Chinese or Japanese might want in exchange. So it made sense to 'test the market' by taking a variety of merchandise.

The largest ship in the fleet was manned and provisioned by the King. It was probably under the personal command of John Cabot. The other vessels from Bristol were said to be 'small ships', albeit that may only be by way of comparison. Henry VII's account books confirm that he invested in the voyage, providing loans totalling £113 8s. to Thomas Bradley and to Lancelot Thirkill 'for his Shipp going towards the new Ilande'.[5] Bradley was a merchant with connections to both London and Bristol, while Thirkill seems to have been London based.[6] In April 1498 another man, John Cair, 'goying to the newe Ile', was given a free gift of 40 shillings by the King.[7]

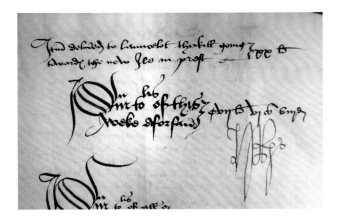

Plate 35 | Payment of £20 to Lancelot Thirkill 'going towardes the new Ile', March 1498; Henry VII signs off the payments for the week with his initials 'HR' (*TNA, E101/414/16, fo. 20v*)

What happened to Cabot remains a mystery. A letter written on 20 June 1498 to the Duke of Milan confirms that the ships had left and that Brother Giovanni Antonio de Carbonariis, whom the Duke knew well, had gone with them. On 25 July, the Spanish Ambassador also recorded the departure of the fleet in a letter to his sovereigns, adding that the ship carrying Carbonariis had been damaged in a storm and forced to land in Ireland. 'The Genoese', by which the ambassador meant Cabot, had 'kept on his way'. While the expedition was expected to return by the autumn, the author of the Great Chronicle of London noted that 'no tidings' had been received by Michaelmas (29 September) 1498. After these reports, there is nothing.[8]

So what became of Cabot's fleet? Given the lack of definite information about the voyage, it has often been supposed that Cabot was lost at sea. Support for this can be found in the writings of Polydore Vergil, the humanist scholar who from 1502 replaced Carbonariis as papal tax collector. In a draft of his general history of England, written in 1512, Vergil reported that Cabot had sailed with a ship provided by the King to search for new lands in the 'British ocean', but that these proved to be:

> nowhere but on the very bottom of the ocean, to which he is thought to have descended together with his boat, the victim himself of that self-same ocean; since after that voyage he was never seen again anywhere.[9]

The problem with Vergil's account is one common to all the early chronicle sources. Both Vergil and the English accounts confuse the chronology of the expeditions. In Vergil's case, however, the weaknesses are compounded by the fact that he was not even in England at the time of the voyages. So it would be unwise to put too much store on his words, which must have been based on second, or even third-hand, information.

Polydore Virgil, Archdeacon of Wells,
and Prebend of Nonnington in the Church of Hereford.

Pub.^d by J.Thane, Spur Street, Leicester Square.

Plate 36 |
Polydore Vergil
(National Portrait
Gallery)

If Cabot's expedition survived, why are there no records of its return? This is why many assume the expedition ended in disaster. The trouble is that records relating to the Bristol voyages are very patchy. The 1496 expedition only came to light with the discovery of the 'John Day letter' in 1955/6, while evidence has emerged since then of several other successful Bristol expeditions to North America that took place between 1499 and 1508. Until recently nobody knew that these voyages even took place, let alone that they returned. Given how poor the evidence is for any of the Bristol voyages, it is possible that at least part of Cabot's 1498 fleet returned home, but that the evidence for it has not been preserved. This might be true even if the expedition explored a substantial part of the North American coastline. By today's standards that would be a notable achievement: an event to be trumpeted. But by the standards of the time, even a voyage right down the eastern seaboard as far as Florida might not have been regarded as a great success. Such a voyage would merely have demonstrated that the land was not inhabited by rich and civilised peoples with whom the explorers could trade. Indeed, if Cabot's expedition had got as far as the Spanish colonies in the Caribbean, all it would have shown was that, if the Orient's rich empires did lie that way, the route was blocked by the Spanish. This would have been a sore point given that Henry VII's charter to Cabot only extended to lands previously 'unknown to Christians'. Cabot could not claim lands, or continue his exploration, in a region the Spanish had already colonised. Given this, and the King's personal commitment to deepening the alliance with Spain, if the Bristol expedition had

Fig 10 | The 'English coast' of North America depicted in the La Cosa map (1500). The red-and-blue flags represent the royal arms of England

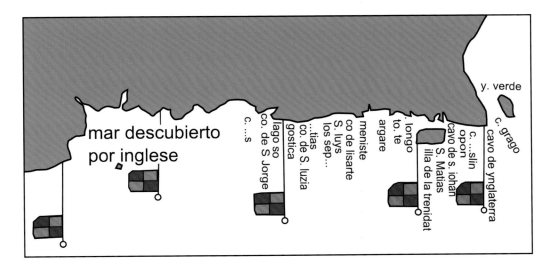

investigated the entire east coast of North America and reached the Caribbean, it would not have been something that either Cabot or the King would have wished to celebrate.

While it is unclear whether the 1498 expedition reached the Caribbean, there are reasons for believing that it did explore further down the coast. The best evidence for this is the world map of Juan de la Cosa drawn in Spain in 1500.[10] This includes the results of the Atlantic discoveries made by the Spanish, Portuguese and English, as illustrated in the introduction to this book. Bristol's contribution is reflected in the five English flags placed along the North American coast. Features are named for the most easterly section of this coast. They seem to be Spanish renditions of English names. While not all are now legible, these include 'Cavo de ynglaterra' (Cape of England), 'Cavo de S: Jorge' (Cape of St George) and 'Cavo de lisarte' (Cape of [the] Lizard). The last was presumably named after its supposed similarity to the Lizard Peninsula, a famous landmark on the southernmost tip of Cornwall.

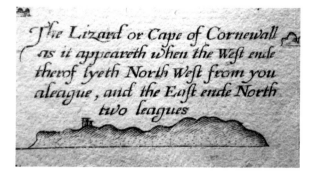

Plate 37 | Profile of the 'The Lizard', taken from a book of sailing directions, *The Mariners Mirrour* (1588)[11]

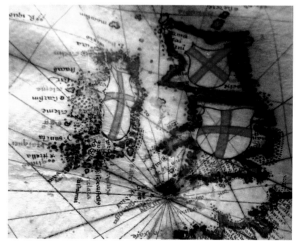

Plate 38 | The focus of rhumb lines on the Cornish Lizard indicates its importance to sailors as a navigation landmark (*Bodleian Library, MS K1 (111)*)

The two western flags define an unnamed coast but are accompanied by a caption indicating that this was the *'mar descubierto por inglese'* (the sea discovered by the English).

The inclusion of specific place names for coastal features implies that la Cosa took his information from an English chart. That would not have been difficult given that the Spanish certainly had copies of at least some of the maps made by Cabot. In July 1498 the Spanish Ambassador in London reported to his sovereigns that he had seen and discussed Cabot's findings with Henry VII 'several times', but that:

> *Since I believe Your Highnesses will already have notice of all this and also of the chart or mappa mundi which this man [Cabot] has made I do not send it now, although it is here*[12]

The named section of the North American coastline on la Cosa's map is most likely based on Cabot's map. On the other hand, the lack of place names for the area to the west implies that, while la Cosa believed that this coast had been explored, he did not have a chart of these discoveries. What is unclear is whether this implied second voyage is the one undertaken by Cabot in 1498, or whether it refers to the 1499 expedition undertaken by William Weston, which will be discussed later.

Plate 39 | Juan de la Cosa's World Map, hand drawn on parchment taken from a single ox hide, 181 cm wide. The 'New World' is the solid green, drawn at an enlarged scale, at the 'neck' end of the skin

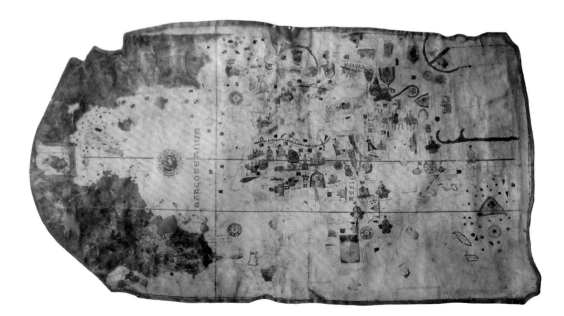

Another hint that the 1498 expedition may have reached the Caribbean can be found in a Spanish royal patent issued in June 1501. This was granted to Alonso de Ojeda for his exploration of the north coast of South America. In the patent, Ojeda was instructed to set up marks along the coast he explored 'because it goes towards the region where it has been learned that the English were making discoveries'. The hope was that such marks would 'stop the exploration of the English in that direction.'[13] This suggests that the Spanish believed that the Bristol expeditions had got close to the region. Such concerns are unlikely to have been aroused by the 1497 expedition, which had taken place far to the north. It seems more likely that the Spanish officials believed that one or more of the later expeditions from Bristol had sailed much further south. But whether this related to the 1498 expedition, or the 1499 one, we do not know.[14]

If the outcome of the 1498 voyage is not already uncertain enough, another element has been added to the mystery in recent years. This concerns the claims of the historian Dr Ruddock, who was mentioned earlier. Although all her research notes were destroyed following her death in 2005, a book proposal she wrote in 1992 survives. In it, she suggests that Cabot reached the Caribbean in 1498 before eventually returning to England in 1500, after a gap of almost two years. Ruddock also implied that she had evidence that the Italian friars, including both Carbonariis and a mysterious 'friar from Naples', succeeded in establishing a religious colony on Newfoundland, complete with North America's first church, at a place that later became known as 'Carbonear'.[15] If so, the friars' ship must have been repaired after the damage it sustained at the start of the 1498 expedition, which had forced it to land in Ireland. Once any problems had been addressed, the ship could have set sail once more, following in Cabot's wake.

Over the last few years, the authors of this book have relocated a number of the 'new documents' on which Ruddock's arguments were based, including references from the summer of 1500 that could relate to Cabot's return.[16] Nothing, however, has been learnt of Carbonariis' fate, and we have not been able to confirm Ruddock's most remarkable claims about this expedition.[17] For now then, the outcome of Cabot's last voyage remains a mystery. Was the entire expedition lost at sea? Possibly. Was a religious mission established in Newfoundland? Perhaps. Did at least part of Cabot's expedition return to England? Quite likely. Right now, however, the outcome of the expedition remains an enigma.

7 BRISTOL AND THE 'NEW FOUND LAND': 1499-1508 VOYAGES

Bristol's exploration voyages to North America, and the King's support for them, did not end with Cabot's 1498 expedition. Over the next ten years the port's merchants undertook several voyages to North America, and created a company to make money from their discoveries.

The first of the 'post-Cabot' expeditions was in 1499, led by the Bristol merchant, William Weston. This probably took place under Cabot's patent, since Weston had been associated with the explorer from the start of 1498, at the latest. The very existence of this voyage was only established in 2009, with the publication of a letter found more than thirty years earlier by Margaret Condon. The letter, apparently written on 12 March 1499, was sent by Henry VII to his Lord Chancellor ordering the suspension of legal proceedings against William Weston, merchant of Bristol, because he shall 'shortly...passe and saille for to serche and fynde if he can the new founde land'.[1] On his return Weston received a £30 reward from the King to help cover the expenses incurred in finding 'the new

Plate 40 | The 'Weston letter'. Signed at the top by the King with his initials (HR), this is the earliest known reference to a post-Cabot voyage of discovery (*TNA: C82/332*)

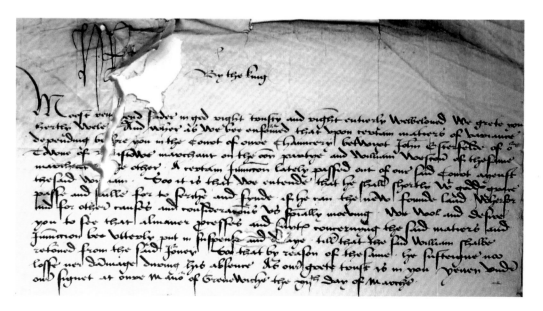

land', thereby confirming that the voyage took place.[2] At this time, 'finding' had a broader meaning than it does today. It could refer to both 'discovering for the first time' and 'investigating something further'. This wider usage was necessary because the words 'explore' and 'exploration' did not enter the English language till the mid-sixteenth century.[3] In his letter of 12 March, the King seems a little uncertain about Weston's abilities. So when the King talked of Weston going to 'fynde' the new land, he might have meant both 'relocate' and 'examine further'. In awards made to Bristol's merchants between 1500 and 1509, it is much clearer that those recompensed for 'finding' the 'new found land', were being rewarded for ongoing investigation, not first discovery. These voyages are discussed below.

Where the 1499 voyage went is unclear: but Alwyn Ruddock, who also knew of these documents, believed Weston went first to the friars' settlement in 'Carbonear', Newfoundland. She suggests that he then headed north up the coast of Labrador as far as the entrance to Hudson Bay, accompanied by the friars' ship, which she identified as the *Dominus Nobiscum*. Such a voyage would have taken the expedition into ice-filled seas, along a barely inhabited coastline. The only plausible explanation for a search this way was that the explorers were looking for a northern route around the landmass. If so, this was not only the first English-led expedition to America, it would also have been the first of the many 'Northwest Passage' expeditions to take place over the next few centuries.

Fig 11 | Course of Weston's voyage, based on Ruddock

Meanwhile, Cabot's death, whether in the New World or, as Alwyn Ruddock believed, shortly after a return to England, left a vacuum. As Columbus discovered in Spain, a monopoly was only a monopoly so long as a monarch chose to uphold it. But the English voyages raised wider issues. According to the Treaty of Tordesillas (1494), concluded between Spain and Portugal, but with the implicit backing of the Pope, Portugal claimed the right to all newly discovered lands that lay east of a meridian starting 370 leagues west of the Cape Verde islands.[4] The Portuguese were convinced that the new lands discovered from Bristol belonged to them. And since Henry VII had assured the Spanish ambassador in 1498 that the territories found by Cabot were not west of the Tordesillas line, he could not now claim that they were not to the east of it.[5] Until this time, the main thrust of Portuguese discovery had been down Africa and towards India. Having learnt what the English were doing, King Manoel of Portugal decided to dispatch his own explorers to the regions discovered by the English: regions, he felt, belonged to Portugal.

Plate 41 | Coat of Arms of King Manoel I of Portugal (*Arquivo Nacional Torre do Tombo, Foral do Casal de Álvaro e Bolfar, PT/ TT/FC/001/344*). Variants of these arms appear on contemporary maps showing lands discovered and claimed for Portugal [6]

In October 1499 and May 1500 King Manoel granted two letters patent for westwards discovery, the first to João Fernandes, of whom we shall hear more later, and the second to Gaspar Corte Real. Of the two, Corte Real moved faster. He undertook two expeditions: the first, in 1500, resulted in the rediscovery of Greenland, albeit he only charted its southern tip. On the second voyage, in 1501, he again touched Greenland but then went on to chart parts of Newfoundland and the Canadian east coast. It may have been on this trip that he planted, in contrast to Cabot's fragile flags, a carved stone marker known as a padrão, of the type that had way-marked Portuguese expansion along the coast of Africa, claiming the land for the King.[7] On one or other of the voyages it seems likely that he commenced a search for a north-west passage.

Gaspar Corte Real was lost in the course of the 1501 expedition, yet his voyages are important to the story of the Bristol expeditions for three reasons. First, it is possible that Gaspar recovered evidence of Cabot's final voyage, since two of the 'indians' he sent to Lisbon were adorned with European goods – a broken sword and earrings. The Venetian ambassador in Lisbon, who witnessed their arrival, interpreted this as evidence that the new land was mainland, so implying that the artefacts were trade goods. Given that this would have been impossible in practice, some historians have argued that the sword and earrings might have been acquired from Cabot's 1498 expedition. Second, Corte Real's survey was preserved in a succession of maps of 1502 and later years. This meant that his charts and the place names he assigned to the coast became the basis for later mapmakers, rather than Cabot's earlier chart.[8] Finally, it was almost certainly because João Fernandes had effectively been side-lined by Corte Real's expeditions that he decided to abandon Portugal and offer his services, along with two other men from the Azores, to the King of England.

The successful voyage of 1497, the King's solid support for the expedition of 1498, and the more limited assistance given to Weston, showed that Henry VII was interested in discovery and the exploitation of new lands. Henry did not accept the validity of a Portuguese claim to lands they had neither discovered nor occupied, whatever the Pope or the monarchs of Castile and Portugal decreed. As far as Henry was concerned, so long as the lands found were 'unknown to all Christians', as Cabot's and subsequent letters patent stipulated, they could be claimed for England. Indeed, in an extraordinary clause included in letters patent of 1501 and 1502, Henry's patentees were permitted to 'wage war' on any foreigner violently intruding into lands discovered on behalf of the King of England.[9]

On 19 March 1501 new letters patent were issued jointly to three Bristol merchants, Richard Warde, Thomas Asshehurst and John Thomas, and to three foreigners, who, as residents of the Azores, were subjects of the King of Portugal. These men were

Plate 42 | The extraordinary 'Cantino' world map of 1502, by an unknown cartographer, incorporates secret information that was 'hot off the press' from Corte Real's expedition. This detail from the map shows both the southern tip of Greenland and, to the left, the section of the forested Canadian coast Corte Real had explored. Like Cabot, he remarked on the suitability of native trees for ship masts.

João Fernandes, Francisco Fernandes and João Gonçalves. The patent was a much more detailed and sophisticated document than the 1496 grant to Cabot. The text occupies nine pages of print in a modern transcript of the original Latin, to Cabot's one and a half. The product of extensive discussions with the King and Council, the grant gave the syndicate vice-regal powers in lands they might discover, a monopoly on trade for ten years, and the ability to assign both their rights and grant licences to trade to other merchants. The patent also gave the holders the right for four years to bring back one ship from any voyage customs free, laden with products of the land: gold, silver and jewels were listed as likely products.[10] The explorers were to receive their patent without paying any of the usual fees, further demonstrating the King's commitment.[11] As with Cabot's 1496 patent, that of March 1501 specified that the explorers would only have rights to lands 'unknown to all Christians'. It thus excluded the territories explored by the Spanish, those discovered by Cabot's patent holders and the parts of the coast of Canada and Greenland that had been investigated by Corte Real the previous year.

It seems that at least one voyage took place in 1501.[12] As with Weston's 1499 voyage, no description of it survives. Yet there is good financial evidence that an expedition occurred and that the

King was pleased with the result. Around 7 January 1502 Henry VII granted a reward of 100 shillings (£5), to the 'men of Bristolle that founde thisle'. This came from the King's personal treasury. The same day an order was sent to the officers of the King's Exchequer for a 'tally' to be made out in favour of the Bristol merchants Robert Thorne, his brother William and Hugh Eliot. The tally allowed the merchants to claim a £20 deduction from customs duties payable on goods brought to the port on the first inward voyage of the *Gabriel*. This was a ship the merchants had recently bought second-hand in Dieppe.[13] The *Gabriel*, of around 120 tuns burden, sailed at least twice to North America after January 1502, and there is copious evidence that Robert Thorne and Hugh Eliot were heavily involved in the later Bristol voyages. Indeed, Robert Thorne junior, writing in 1527, described his father and Eliot as the 'discoverers of the Newfound Landes', which raises the possibility that they had been involved since Cabot's time. At any rate, given that the reward in January 1502 was paid on the same day that the King's warrant authorising the customs deduction was sealed, it seems highly probable that the two Thornes and Eliot were 'the men of Bristolle' who had undertaken a 1501 voyage acting as assigns or deputies of those who were granted the March 1501 patent.[14]

More is known of the voyage made in 1502, which certainly took place under the terms of the 1501 patent. Hugh Eliot sailed in the *Gabriel* as an 'assign' of the patentees. It seems likely that at least one other ship sailed with her, albeit none is recorded by name. The explorers returned to Bristol in September 1502, just too late to find the King at nearby Berkeley Castle. They were thus forced to follow Henry to his hunting lodge at King's Langley, Hertfordshire.[15] There, they found favour: on 26 September 1502, pensions of £10 per year, payable from the customs of Bristol, were granted to both Francisco Fernandes and João Gonçalves for the services they had given as 'captains into the new found land'.[16] These services probably included the bringing back of three 'savage men', who were said to be clothed in beasts' skins and ate raw flesh. The three Native Americans seem to have been taken into the King's household, one commentator noting that two years later he:

> saw two of them apparelled after [the manner of] *Englishmen in Westminster Palace, which at that time I could not discern* [i.e. tell them apart] *from Englishmen, till I learned what men they were.*[17]

A series of European charts, commencing from about 1503, ascribe the discovery of lands that can be interpreted either as the north-east coast of Canada, or Greenland, to a 'labrador' in the service of the King of England. A 'labrador' in this context means a landowner from the Azores. This discovery too seems likely to date from the 1502 voyage and is consistent with the exotic goods brought back as gifts for Henry VII.[18] In mid to late September, books of the King's personal treasury report that two mariners had brought Henry hawks and an eagle. This was followed, about a week later, by a reward of £20 to 'the merchauntes of bristoll that have bene in the newe founde landes'. The merchants undoubtedly included Hugh Eliot, and possibly Robert Thorne.[19] Eliot himself was granted a pension of twenty marks (£13 6s 8d) and it was he who took advantage of the right, permitted by their patent, to import a single lading of merchandise from the new land free of custom. The *Gabriel*, mastered by John Amayne, had brought back 18 lasts of salt fish (54 tons), worth £180 by customs valuations. The tax due on this would have been £9.[20] Although this was a significant quantity of fish, the consignment was not large enough for the venture to have been entirely a fishing voyage. The limited size of the catch, set against the generous scale of the King's response, indicates that the 1502 voyage was primarily a voyage of exploration.

Plate 43 | "'Tiera de Llabrador' which was discovered by the English from the town of Bristol..." Ribeiro map, 1529: (from Nordenskiöld, Periplus: original in Vatican Library)[21]

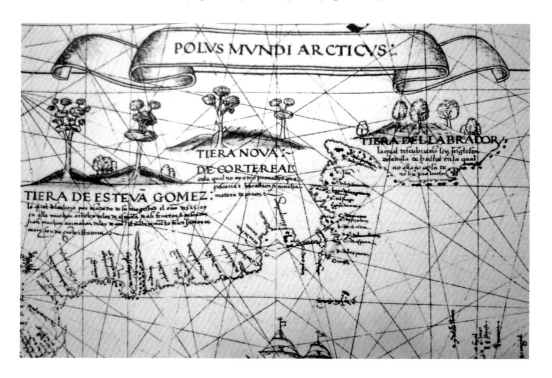

Despite the apparent success of the 1502 expedition, there were signs of fracture in the partnership. Whether this was by death or disagreement is unknown. By this time Henry VII must have been aware of Corte Real's explorations and if the King were to make claims to lands based on 'first discovery' he had to acknowledge that the doctrine of primacy worked both ways: the King of Portugal now had a claim to lands in the region. The changed situation required a new grant, which was issued on 9 December 1502 to a revised group of patentees: Hugh Eliot, Thomas Asshehurst, Francisco Fernandes and João Gonçalves.[22] The tone of this patent is darker, making reference to the great costs and heavy dangers of any expedition, and the terms were consequently more generous. This time, the rights of the King of Portugal were specifically protected, as were those of any other prior discovery by servants of other powers in friendship with England.[23]

The new patent, like its predecessor, was very detailed, with explicit provisions allowing for the sale of shares in the patent to third parties. In effect the grant created something very like a chartered monopoly company of the type that would become common in the later sixteenth century. The group became known as the 'Company Adventurers to the New Found Land'. The use of the name 'adventurers' is particularly significant, in that this was the term used for merchants who engaged in speculative long-distance commerce. It seems that the explorers still expected to get their money back through trade.

Whether there were any English expeditions in 1503 is uncertain. In September the King received a 'brasil bow' and two red arrows whilst he was on progress in the Midlands, and he was given hawks 'from the newe founden Ilande' in November.[24] It seems likely these were the fruits of a voyage undertaken that summer: but further detail is absent.

In 1504 there was an expedition about which we would dearly like to know more, since it appears to have been the first to engage Sebastian Cabot, John Cabot's son, in a leading role. Two ships were involved: the *Gabriel* of Bristol, mastered by Philip Ketyner, and the *Jesus*, under Richard Savery. Hugh Eliot and his long-term business partner, Robert Thorne, and Robert's brother, William, seem to have been the principal organisers. Eliot led the expedition, with Sebastian Cabot probably serving as pilot.[25] They must have sailed rather later than was usual, perhaps as late as June, since Richard Savery only returned around 20 May from a commercial voyage to Bordeaux.[26] Robert Thorne was unable to join them: in early 1504 the town council had made him a sheriff of Bristol, following the unexpected death of one of the two serving officers. While prestigious, it was a demanding role, which leading citizens were frequently forced to take on. Whether or not Robert was pleased by the development, his new legal duties would have precluded exploration on the far side of the Atlantic.

Plate 44 | Bristol's sheriff and law officers
(Ricart's Kalendar, Bristol Record Office)[27]

Given that Sebastian would have inherited his father's patent rights, his participation in the voyage suggests that all those who had been engaged in Bristol's expeditions since 1496 were now working together. This time, the ships' passengers included a priest, who may have been fired by the same missionary zeal that had inspired Carbonariis and the Italian friars in 1498.[28] Around Easter Sunday (7 April 1504), the unnamed priest received a good-will gift from the King of forty shillings for his journey to the 'new Ilande'.[29] As with Hugh Eliot's 1502 expedition, we only know of the ships used on the 1504 voyage because of the customs exemption granted by the terms of the revised patent of 1502. In this instance the consignment brought from the 'Newe Found Ilande' amounted to 20 lasts of salted fish and 7 and a half tons of fish livers.[30] Again, while not insignificant, the shipment (67 tons) did not represent anything like a full loading for two vessels that had a combined cargo capacity of about 250 tons. Fishing thus apparently remained a side activity, rather than being the primary function of the voyage.

What would have interested the King was the exploration aspect of the Bristol voyages, with their potential to open up valuable new trade routes, or find commodities as the Portuguese and Spanish had done. It was almost certainly to support such aims that a reward of £100 was made at about this time towards the cost of an expedition to the new found isle in two ships.[31] On the other hand, Henry also seems to have been attracted, like many others at this time, by the sheer novelty of the new world and its exotic products. He certainly saw presentations by Cabot, describing the lands he had found; and the King was clearly pleased by both the new animals he was brought and by three native Americans, whom the King treated relatively well by the standards of the day, giving them a place in his court. Such pleasure was demonstrated again in the week of 10 August 1505, when some 'Portyngales' (Portuguese) were rewarded for bringing the King 'cattes of the mountaigne' and 'popyngayes of the newfounde Island' for his royal menagerie. It is unclear whether this followed yet another Bristol expedition, about which we know nothing, or whether they were a gift from Portugal.[32] While the 'popinjays' (parrots) could have been Carolina parakeets, by 1502 Brazil was also known for its highly-coloured birds.

Within a few years, the merchants and explorers who had been brought together in 1502 seem to have fallen out. In 1506 William Clerk of London sued Hugh Eliot in relation to a number of alleged debts, including expenses he had incurred for a 'voyage of the Company Adventurers prepared into the new found lands'. Around the same time Francisco Fernandes, who was one of the Portuguese named in the 1502 patent, appealed to the King in the Court of Chancery following his imprisonment in Bristol for non-payment of a £100 debt to Eliot. The Portuguese claimed not only that he did not owe the money but that Eliot actually owed him money.[33] These court cases suggest that there was much 'bad blood' between the members of the Company, presumably rooted in their failure to either make a profit, or to identify a route to the Orient.

It is possible that the Company Adventurers to the New Found Land dissolved around 1505/6 and that the legal disputes relate to its final break up. There was, however, one last voyage from Bristol during the reign of Henry VII, this time led and organised by Sebastian Cabot. As already observed, Sebastian had certainly taken part in the expedition of 1504 and on 3 April 1505 the King granted him a pension of £10 per year, to be received out of the customs revenue collected at Bristol for services 'in and aboute the fyndynge of the newe founde lands to oure full good pleasur and for that he shall doo hereafter in and aboute the same'. It was backdated to the previous Michaelmas (29 September 1504).[34]

Unlike the voyages that took place from 1499-c1506, various accounts of Sebastian's voyage survive, based on the explorer's own version of events. The problem is that Sebastian was not an entirely reliable witness. Indeed, in his later life, he started claiming that it was he, rather than his father, who had first discovered the new world, which is why John Cabot was largely written out of English discovery history from the late-sixteenth century to the mid-nineteenth century.[35] It is also why, when it was finally

Plate 45 | Sebastian Cabot: engraving by Samuel Rawle from a now lost portrait[36]

established that John had in fact led the expeditions of the 1490s, Sebastian went from being a 'hero' to a 'villain' of English discovery history: branded a 'liar and a charlatan' by late-Victorian writers, for claiming his father's achievements.[37] Sebastian was, however, a notable explorer in his own right.

As a navigator and promoter of exploration voyages, Sebastian's main interest was to talk-up his personal achievements as a way of bolstering his own reputation. So his voyage accounts cannot be taken at face value. Nevertheless, they should not be written off entirely. In particular, some credence should be given of his story of a voyage apparently undertaken in 1508-9, particularly given the earliest description of it was penned just a few years after it took place, when there were still many other people around who could have gainsaid him. That Sebastian was absent from England in 1508 is almost certain, since he did not collect the first instalment of his pension for that year until May 1509.[38]

The first account of the voyage, published in 1516 by his friend, Peter Martyr of Anghiera, suggests that Sebastian had led a voyage involving two ships and 300 men.[39] The expedition started by sailing north along the American coastline until, in July, they found their way blocked by great icebergs. Based on some later accounts, Cabot may have got as far as Hudson Bay.[40] He then headed south, passed through the rich cod fisheries that lie off the coast of Newfoundland and New England, and continued on until he was 'almost in the latitude of Gibraltar' and 'almost the longitude of Cuba'. This would

Plate 46 | It is likely that Sebastian used an astrolabe to establish his latitude (*Photo: Shutterstock*)

suggest that he reached as far as the Chesapeake, close to what is now Washington D.C. Following this he sailed back to England. Although Peter Martyr's earliest account does not give the date of the voyage, in later writings he indicated that the voyage had taken place around 1508/9. This is supported by an unrelated report made before the Venetian Senate in the 1530s, which states that, when Sebastian returned to England at the end of this voyage, 'he found the King dead, and his son cared little for such an enterprise.'[41] Given that Henry VII died in April 1509, it seems likely that the voyage had started in the summer of 1508, with the expedition over-wintering on the East Coast of the modern United States before returning home.

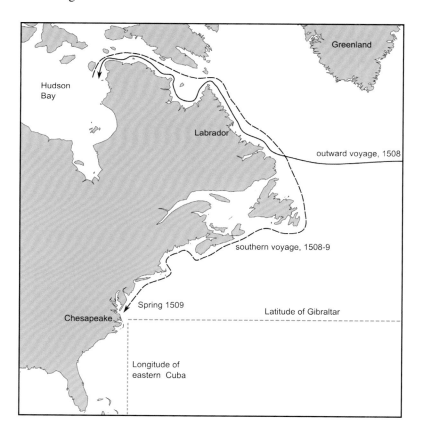

Fig 12 | Presumed course of Sebastian Cabot's voyage of 1508-9

Sebastian's expedition was the last exploration voyage to be launched from Bristol during the Tudor era. It may be that Bristol's merchants had become disillusioned after repeatedly funding expeditions that had brought only modest returns, and which had certainly not found gold, spices or a route to the Orient. Moreover, Sebastian's final English expedition appears to have resulted in the death of a large part of the crew. Beyond this, it was certainly the case that Henry VIII proved much less interested in promoting discovery voyages than his father, as the later report to the Venetian Senate implies. Indeed, while Henry VII has a reputation for being rather mean with money, one of the chief outcomes of the research conducted over the last fifty years has been to show that the King maintained an active interest in the Bristol voyages throughout the latter part of his reign: offering money, political support and administrative interventions to ensure they continued. By contrast, his son was more interested in conquering old territories in France than he was in finding new ones across the Ocean. The result was that, while there were some voyages to North America in Henry VIII's reign, they were modest affairs, and they no longer involved Bristol.[42] It seems likely that it was this decline in interest from both the new king and the merchants of Bristol that explains why Sebastian decided to leave England for Spain in 1512. There he subsequently played an important part in Spain's endeavour to explore and colonise the Americas.

8 THE NAMING OF THE LAND

When John Cabot and his Bristol companions returned to England in 1497 they did not seek to name their newly discovered land. Christopher Columbus named his Caribbean discoveries after Spain (Hispaniola), for his sovereigns (Isabella), and for God (Trinidad). But in England the area explored by Cabot was described at first only as the 'new isle' or 'new Ilande', while after 1499 it was also known as the 'new found ilande' or the 'new founde lande'.[1] The last of these was the name that stuck, with Newfoundland now being the name of the great island off the coast of Canada. But this does not mean that all sixteenth-century references to the 'new found land' refer to the island. For a long time the 'new found land' simply meant what it said: it was the land discovered and explored from Bristol in the years 1497–1508. Although this included the modern island, it encompassed a much wider area.

Cabot charted his discoveries in 1497 and incorporated them in a *mappa mundi* and globe he exhibited to the King. While neither Cabot's original charts nor his world map survives, his findings were integrated into Juan de la Cosa's Spanish *mappa mundi* of 1500. Neither La Cosa's map, nor any of the statements made by Cabot or his contemporaries, suggest that the explorer invented a new name for the country. That was probably because it seemed unnecessary. When Cabot returned in 1497 he told people that the region belonged to the Emperor of China. He further suggested that some of the country was the land of the 'Seven Cities', a name that was included in the La Cosa map and had appeared on world maps for at least two centuries. The following year Cabot planned to sail down the coast to China and Cipango (Japan). Once he had done that he probably assumed that he would learn from the rich and civilised peoples of those countries just what they called the territory he found in 1497. So naming this land, as opposed to charting the coast and assigning names to navigational landmarks, probably seemed superfluous.

Over the next century the continents and countries of the Americas would be known by many names. While lots of these are still used today, both the form of each name and the geographical limit to which it applies has often changed. The islands explored by Columbus, for instance, were initially simply called the 'Indies', because he believed them to be part of Asia. It was only much later, when it became clear that this was wrong, that the name transmuted to the 'West Indies'.

The most important new name for the discoveries across the Atlantic was, of course, 'America'. While this name has nothing to do with Bristol, its origin is worth discussing. That is because of a persistent Bristol myth that America is named after a Bristol customs officer called Richard 'Ameryk'.

There are many uncertainties in the field of discovery history. But the origin of the name 'America' is not one of them. The two continents get their name from the Florentine navigator Amerigo Vespucci (1454-1512): a man with as many careers as John Cabot, and an inveterate self-publicist. He was also a successful explorer who, unlike Cabot, published accounts of his voyages. These accounts proved extremely popular in the early sixteenth century for their vivid descriptions of exotic landscapes, peoples and wildlife. Vespucci was also known for being the first to propose that the new discoveries were not a part of Asia, but were instead a genuinely 'New World'.[2] This put him at odds with Columbus, who was still arguing up until his death in 1506 that the lands were part of the Orient.

A few years after the publication of his chief works, Vespucci was honoured by two German scholars: the humanist Matthias Ringmann, and Martin Waldseemüller, a monk who was a skilled printer and mapmaker. In their *Cosmographiae Introductio* of 1507, they proposed a new continent or 'fourth part of the world':

> *Today these parts of the earth* [Asia, Europe, Africa] *have been more extensively explored than a fourth part of the world ... that has been discovered by Amerigo Vespucci. Because it is well known that Europe and Asia were named after women, I can see no reason why anyone would have good reason to object to calling this fourth part Amerige, the land of Amerigo, or America, after the man of great ability who discovered it.*[3]

The large twelve-sheet map that Waldseemüller created to illustrate their text attempts to show the world as a sphere.[4] Martin Waldseemüller placed the name 'America' prominently on what we would now call South America. In the top border of the map, Waldseemüller included portraits of Vespucci and the great classical cosmographer, Claudius Ptolemy, and small half-globes showing the old world and the new continent.[5] Comments printed on the map pay tribute to both Columbus and Vespucci, and to their royal patrons.[6]

Plate 47 | Amerigo Vespucci with Asia and the New World from the Waldseemüller map. Most of North America is unexplored: the detached island at the top we know to be Corte Real's discoveries *(Library of Congress)*

Waldseemüller's map was soon forgotten.[7] But the *Cosmographiae Introductio* proved influential; and Waldseemüller's and Ringmann's use of the name 'America' was picked up by other cartographers and scholars.[8] The name became widely adopted as the umbrella term to describe the southern continent, but it only began to be used to describe the northern continent in the second half of the sixteenth century, two generations after the exploration voyages of Columbus and Cabot. For their part, Bristol's merchants, along with other Englishmen, used the term 'new found land' to describe the country they had explored. That was true in the first decade of the sixteenth century, when the 'Company Adventurers to the Newfound land' was founded; it was true in 1523 when Robert Thorne of Bristol boasted that his father was one of 'the discoverers of the Newfound Landes'; and it was true in the 1560s when Bristol's merchants complained to the Queen that 'theyre oft attempted voyages to the newfoundland' had given them little profit.[9] The term 'America' does not seem to have been used to describe the Bristol discoveries until the 1560s and then only rarely.

There is then a great deal of evidence that the continent of South America was named for Amerigo Vespucci, including statements to this effect by the men who coined the term. By contrast, there is no evidence that the term was used to describe the lands to the north until the later sixteenth century, when the vast extent of the northern land-mass, and that it was joined to the southern continent, was better understood. Before then, Bristol men, the royal administration, and even French mariners, preferred to use 'New found land' for the discovery, while the Spanish tended to refer to the North American territories they explored and settled after 1513 as 'New Spain' or 'Florida'.

So why should anyone propose that the new continent was named after a Bristol customs official? The answer seems to be that many people simply 'want' this to be true. This myth began with a Bristol antiquarian, Alfred Hudd, who published a document in 1897 that he called the 'Cabot Roll'.

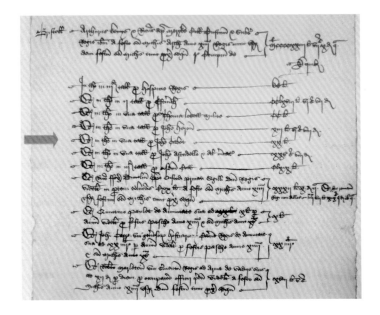

Plate 48 | Payment by Arthur Kemys and Richard ap Meryke of Cabot's pension 1498-9 from 'The Cabot Roll'. Cabot's £20 (xx li.) is just one of the eleven payments on this page.[10]

Hudd's book provides a facsimile, Latin transcription and English translation, of an official document that summarises the audited accounts of the customs officers of the port of Bristol for a three-year period. For each year, the document lists the payments made from the money that the Collectors of Customs had received on behalf of the Crown. These include the payment of John Cabot's English pension from 1497-1499.[11] The two 'Collectors of Customs' at Bristol were Arthur Kemys and the Welshman, Richard Ap Meryk. In those days spelling was not formalised and people did not worry about the precise form of either first names or surnames. It is thus not unusual that Ap Meryk's name is recorded in many different ways in contemporary documents: including 'A Merik', 'ap Meryke', 'Meryk', 'Meurik' and 'Ameryke'. Hudd noticed that some variants of the customs officer's name resembled the name 'America'. On this slender basis he proposed in 1908 that John Cabot might have named the continent after the customer.[12]

Plate 49 | Richard ap Meryk: contemporary name variants. The first names are abbreviations of the latin forms for Richard; the surnames read: a Meryk, Meryk, a merik, ap meryke, Amerik, meurik, and Apmerike.[13]

The Welsh name Ap Meryk means 'son of Meryk', (or 'Meurig') in the same way that Fitzpatrick means 'son of Patrick' and Macdonald 'son of Donald'. As with other patronymics, such names had become common surnames by the fifteenth century. Richard Ap Meryk was said to be from Chepstow in Monmouthshire, but like many aspiring Welshmen, he moved to Bristol.[14] He made his money through trade and by at least the mid-1470s had begun to acquire a landed estate that would give him status as a gentleman.[15] In August 1486 he was appointed as one of the two 'customers' of Bristol, responsible for collecting dues payable to the Crown on merchandise passing through the port. He retained this office until December 1502.[16] Nine months later, he became one of Bristol's sheriffs. His appointment was meant to last from 29 September 1503 – 29 September 1504, but he died suddenly around December, only three months into his term.[17]

In October 1493 Ap Meryk had been joined as customer by Arthur Kemys, who had previously been 'controller' in the port.[18] Controllers were employed to keep an independent record of the goods declared at the customs house, with the sole purpose of preventing a customer from defrauding the Crown. For example, a customer might under-charge merchants for their goods, in return for a bribe. He might also falsify records after duty had been paid, recording lower figures in his books and pocketing the difference. In 1489, and repeatedly in the 1490s, Ap Meryk was charged with malpractice. His alleged offences included engagement in foreign trade, which was forbidden for customs officers, sharp practice, and falsification of records. He eventually avoided a guilty verdict and retained his office. That, however, was only because the local juries proved reluctant to convict. This was a common problem at the time, even when the evidence was overwhelming, and does not mean that Ap Meryk was innocent – a point underlined by the fact that one set of legal proceedings ended only after he negotiated directly with the King and agreed to pay a £100 fine. That was equivalent to almost two years of his official income, or five times as much as John Cabot's annual pension.[19] The case against Ap Meryk must have been strong.

Ap Meryk's only known association with John Cabot is his responsibility, shared with Kemys, for the payment of the explorer's pension from the customs revenues collected at Bristol. This does not demonstrate any special relationship between the two: the funds collected from customs dues belonged to the Crown and it was perfectly normal for the King to pay people's salaries and pensions from such local funds. Indeed, of the two men, Kemys had the more personal association, in that his nephew, John Kemys,

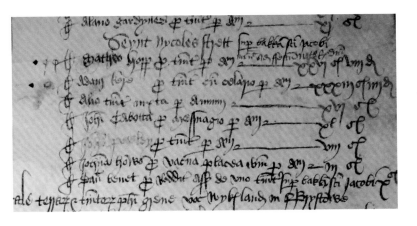

Plate 50 | The annual rent of 40 shillings payable in 1498-9 by John 'Cabotta' for a house (messuage) on 'Seynt Nycoles Strett' is the most expensive in this short list for the street (Gloucestershire Archives, D674/a/Z9)

owned the property on St Nicholas Street that John Cabot rented when he lived in Bristol.[20] This though was a very slight connection, in that John Kemys was a minor, whose estate was managed by his guardian, and future father-in-law, Philip Grene of Bristol.[21]

The lack of any evidence for a business association between Ap Meryk and Cabot has not stopped local historians from asserting that there was one. For example, it has been said that 'Amerike' helped finance the expeditions and even provided timber for the *Matthew*; and that the grateful explorer then decided to name the land he discovered after his benefactor. There is, unfortunately, no evidence for any of this. When historians wish to establish something, it is not enough to say that 'someone said this in their book'. It is necessary to chase back the references and find the original documents on which any claim is based. In this case that is not possible, because the claims are baseless.

Richard Ap Meryk is an interesting and complex character. Many of his activities are well documented: particularly those that relate to his corrupt practices as a customs officer, and his opportunism in exploiting the financial woes of others in the course of building his landed estate.[22] No evidence has been found, however, to show that he was one of Cabot's supporters, or that he contributed in a positive way to the expeditions. Indeed, if anything, the Bristol customs officers seem to have been an irritation to Cabot, refusing to make the initial payment of his pension in January 1498, even though the King's grant made it clear that this should happen. The officers' objection was, in effect, that Cabot had not acquired all the correct 'paperwork'. While he had a personal order from the King in the form of his letters patent, he had not used this to obtain an authorising warrant acceptable to the exchequer, instructing the customs officers to make the payment. Cabot was thus forced to ride 120 miles back to London to sort the matter out. While the customers' actions were legal, they were neither helpful, nor suggestive of a close personal interest in Cabot.[23] Bristol's customs officers had, in fact, very little to gain from Cabot's success, since the explorer's 1496 patent specified that any trade he established would be customs free. So Kemys and Ap Meryk would not have been able to profit from any trade established, either by collecting official fees for processing goods, or by demanding 'facilitation payments' for doing their jobs in a timely fashion, or for turning a blind eye to smuggling activity.

When all is said and done, there is no evidence that Ap Meryk supported Cabot and little reason why he should have done so. There was no reason why Cabot would have named his new land after Ap Meryk and there is no evidence that he did so. The copies made of Cabot's charts imply that he invented no new name for the lands he explored, while for generations afterwards Bristolians referred to the territories discovered from their port as the 'new found land'. That was true even after 'America' started being used as a term for the northern continent in the second half of the sixteenth century.[24] By contrast, the term 'America' was used to describe continental South America from 1507, when the term was coined by a German mapmaker as an explicit tribute to Amerigo Vespucci.

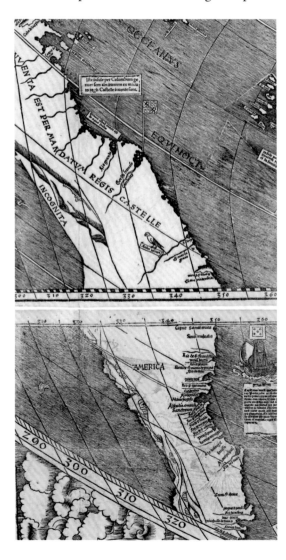

Plate 51 | America south of the Equator on the Waldseemüller map (*Library of Congress*)

9 SHIPS AND SAILORS OF THE DISCOVERY VOYAGES

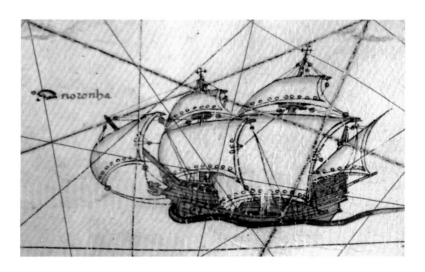

In the Elizabethan period, when Bristol's chroniclers finally became interested in the earlier discovery voyages, they did not remember Cabot. Rather they recalled that it was 'men of Bristol' who had discovered America, in a Bristol ship called the *Matthew*.[1] There was some justice to this view, given that most of the ventures of the period 1496-1508 were led by Bristol men, sailing in Bristol ships. But what was the world of these ships and mariners like?

The 1503/4 customs account for Bristol provides a good sense of the port's fleet in this era.[2] The overseas trade it records was much more typical of the port's maritime activity than voyages of discovery. Bristol ships completed dozens of commercial voyages each year. By contrast, only a few ships were employed for exploration and most of those voyages lasted only a few months. So even ships that were bought for the purpose of exploration, such as the *Gabriel*, spent most of their time ploughing the regular sea-lanes between Bristol, France and Iberia.

In all there were at least 23 vessels in Bristol's fleet, ranging from ships of around 130 tons burden to single-masted boats of perhaps

Ship Name	Type	Size (tons)	Known destinations
Jesus Bonaventure	Small ship	136+ (c.130)	N. America, Bordeaux
Mary Tower	Small ship	128+	Lisbon
Mary Katherine	Small ship	125+	Andalusia, Lisbon, Bordeaux
Gabriel	Small ship	103+ (c.120)	N. America, Andalusia, Bordeaux
Margaret	Small ship	112+	Bordeaux
Mary Belhouse	Small ship	105+	Andalusia, Algarve
Julian Bonaventure	Small ship	79+ (100+)	N. Spain, Bordeaux
Michael	Small ship	72+ (95)	Andalusia, La Rochelle
Trinity	Small ship	-	Bordeaux
Christopher	Small ship	45+	Lisbon, Bordeaux, La Rochelle, Ireland
Julian	Small ship	39+	Lisbon, Bordeaux, Ireland
Matthew	Small ship	34+ (50)	N. Spain, Bordeaux, Ireland
George	Small ship	31+	N. Spain, Bordeaux
Francis	Small ship	30+	Algarve, Ireland
Christopher	Boat	32+	Brittany, Ireland
St Mark	Boat	27+	Portugal, Galicia, N. Spain
Andrew	Small ship	24+	Guernsey
Philip	Boat	22+	La Rochelle, Ireland
Barbara	Boat	23+	Bordeaux, La Rochelle, Ireland
Mary	Small ship/Boat	-	Ireland
Katherine	Boat	-	Ireland
Augustine	Boat	5+	Ireland
Ellen	Boat	2+	Chepstow

Table 1 | Bristol fleet in 1503/4[3]

2-10 tons. The smaller vessels rarely went further than Wales or Ireland, while the greatest ships were used for the long-distance voyages to Spain, Portugal and France. The most famous of the ships listed here is the *Matthew*, which John Cabot used for his 1497 expedition. She bustled between Bristol, Ireland and the Bay of Biscay, carrying a variety of commodities for whoever wanted to charter her. Not all of this trade was legal: smuggled goods were seized from the *Matthew* in November 1498 and then again in 1500.[4] Such versatility made the *Matthew* suitable for the initial exploration voyage of 1497. Being small would have made her fairly cheap to hire and to crew but limited the number of men and provisions she could carry. This may explain why larger ships such as the *Gabriel* and the *Jesus Bonaventure* were used in the later expeditions.

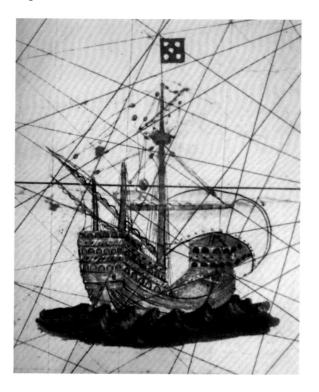

Plate 53 | Portuguese ship from a map of c. 1510

Although there are no detailed depictions of Bristol ships from this period, there are contemporary illustrations of vessels used in the trade of Atlantic Europe, including the 'caravels' and 'naus' that the Spanish and Portuguese favoured for Atlantic exploration. These provide a good sense of what Bristol's ships would have looked like, since the vessels used by English merchants to trade to France, Spain and Portugal were very similar to those used by the merchants of those countries. Indeed, several of Bristol's ships were foreign built. They include two discovery vessels: the *Gabriel*, which was bought from Dieppe in c.1501 and the *Jesus Bonaventure*, which was acquired from the shipyards of St Jean-de-Luz in 1502.[5] Similarly, when the *Matthew* of Bristol went out of commission in 1507, her owner, John Shipman of Bristol, replaced her with a ship built in Spain, which he also called the *Matthew*.[6]

A good modern example of the vessels used for exploration is the reconstruction of the *Matthew* of Bristol, which was built to celebrate the five-hundredth anniversary of Cabot's 1497 expedition. She is a three-masted vessel with square sails on her main and foremast, and a triangular lateen sail on the mizzen (rear) mast, which makes it easier for the ship to tack into the wind. Like most vessels of that period, the modern *Matthew* is 'carvel-built', which means she was built by first constructing a heavy wooden skeleton, on to which planks were then laid edge-to-edge.

Bigger ships, of course, required bigger crews. But they were more efficient, so a ship of 200 tons burden did not need twice as many seaman as one of 100 tons. The fifty-ton *Matthew*'s ordinary complement would have been around thirteen to sixteen men and boys, not counting the master or any merchants on board. For a ship of her size, the rough rule-of-thumb was that one crew member was needed for every 3 to 3.5 tons; a larger ship might only have had one man to every four or five tons of carrying capacity.[8] Even though she took about twenty men on the 1497 voyage, including Cabot himself, the *Matthew* was under-manned by the standards of the Spanish explorers. For example, the Guerra-Grajeda expedition of 1501 allowed 30 mariners and 10 soldiers, not including the

Plate 55 |Bristol's replica ship, the *Matthew*, out 'at sea' in the tidal Severn Estuary *(Photo: Shawn Spencer-Smith)*

gentlemen, for a ship of c. 100 tons, while an accompanying vessel, which was the same size as the *Matthew*, was to carry 23 mariners and 7 soldiers.[9]

Although Cabot was the chief navigator and 'captain' of the *Matthew*, the day-to-day running would have been the responsibility of the shipmaster. Other members of the crew would have included the ship's carpenter, who was responsible for the fabric of the ship, and the bosun, who looked after the sails and rigging. Even small ships like the *Matthew* would also have had a gunner and a few soldiers, to defend her if she were attacked by pirates. By way of armament, she would have carried bows, crossbows and swivel-mounted guns. Such weapons were an essential part of her 'apparel', the marine equivalent of fixtures and fittings.

Most of Bristol's mariners lived in Bristol itself, or at Pill and Shirehampton, about five miles downriver. It was there, in an area

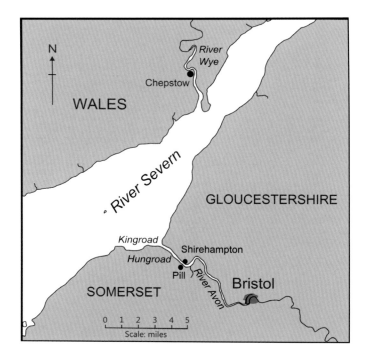

Fig 13 | The River Severn and the ports of Chepstow and Bristol (includes Kingroad)

called the Hungroad, that much of the activity of the port took place: ranging from the loading and unloading of the largest ships, to repair work and the supply of provisions and equipment for voyages. On the other hand, few crews would have been made up entirely of local men. A contemporary business account refers to Bristol ships taking on additional men in Wales, Somerset and Ireland.[10] Mariners were a skilled, specialised and highly mobile profession, who could sell their skills to any master, of any nationality. It would have thus been unusual to find a crew that was made up entirely of Englishmen and some may have come from far-flung destinations. Christopher Columbus' crews in 1492 are well documented, and included a 'negro' and several Portuguese sailors.[11]

While Cabot was probably in his fifties by the time he sailed, most mariners were young, typically in their late teens or twenties, although masters and their deputies might continue into middle age. Most ships also carried a few boys, or 'pages' as they were called in the records. Popular tradition unkindly gave the role of cook to an old sailor no longer fit for active service.[12] Life at sea was hard and required strength, bravery, and great physical toughness. Frequently wet, often cold, even resting was rarely comfortable, with the crews of smaller vessels sleeping on deck, under the covered forecastle.

When the wind blew and the waves rose, a ship like the *Matthew* would be tossed about like a cork, her yards sinking into the foam, while great waves crashed over the decks. In such conditions, sailors had to work on: taking in sail, steering the ship and even climbing frozen rigging at night to reach the crow's nest. In such conditions, one slip would be fatal: those washed into the sea were rarely seen again.

Working at sea required a lot of energy, so while the diet was monotonous, the food allowances were generous. A typical daily diet consisted of 1 lb. of dried ship's biscuit, 2 lb. of salt beef and 10 pints of ale, with cheese and dried fish sometimes taking the place of the beef.[13] In all, this amounted to about 5,000 calories, which is about twice that recommended today for a grown man. If the food was plentiful (and the alcohol allowances more so), there was little variation to the diet, with almost no fresh food, such as fruit, bread or unsalted meat, once a ship had been a week at sea. And much food had to be eaten cold, for heating was only possible when the sea was calm and it was possible to light a fire in a special metal dish that was placed on deck. This made it possible to cook pots of stew that would be served up into the wooden bowls that each sailor kept as one of his prized personal possessions.

Plate 56 |Three of the 188 wooden bowls recovered from the *Mary Rose*, wrecked in 1545 (*Mary Rose Trust*). Food was often first ladled into a large bowl as a 'mess' to be shared between several men; from this, each man could serve his portion into his own bowl.

Although a mariner's life was hard and often dangerous, there were always periods on any voyage when the wind was fair, or absent, when there would be little to do. At those times sailors carried out routine tasks, like mending clothes, or relaxed by playing board games and gambling with dice. The playing pieces recovered from shipwrecks such as the Newport Medieval Ship and the *Mary Rose* would be familiar today.[14] Sailors also had time for entertainment, with singing being a regular feature of an English mariner's life throughout the Age of Sail. Little of their rhymes or 'shanties' survives from the Middle Ages, but, almost uniquely, a fragment of a Bristol mariner's song of Cabot's time survives in a note written down in an idle moment by a local legal clerk. It preserves some of the rhythm of the sailors' teamwork as they hauled on heavy ropes, or pulled on sweeps, and prayed for a fair wind:

> *Hale and howe Rumbylowe*
> *Stire well the gode ship and lete the wynde blowe ....* [15]

10 AFTERMATH

One of the things people today find most difficult to understand about the Bristol discovery voyages is why we know so little about them. Why did so few contemporaries write about the expeditions? The answer is that, however impressive the explorers' exploits might seem today, after the first euphoria, people at the time did not feel they had achieved much of value. Indeed, even if the explorers had succeeded in charting the entire east coast of North America, that would not have been thought terribly important, since America was not what they were looking for. When they set sail, they were hoping to find rich commodities they could bring home, such as brasilwood, or civilised people they could trade with, such as the Chinese.

What Bristol's mariners discovered instead was a wild coastline inhabited by hunter-gatherers and, if they went further south, stone-age farmers. These people had little worth trading, and certainly none of the silk, spices, gold, gems, or dyewood that had been hoped for. Moreover, there was no indication that there were readily extractable resources, such as precious metals. The natives did have land, of course; but the Bristol explorers were not particularly interested in colonisation. In the late-fifteenth century, England was still recovering from the Black Death, with a population half what it had been 150 years earlier. With land cheap and wages high at home, it would have been very difficult to persuade Englishmen to settle in America. The explorers' patents saw settlement as a possibility; but even a hundred years later it was a daunting prospect. All this meant that, to the Bristol explorers, North America was no more than an obstacle blocking the way to Asia. To them, discovering America was probably a bitter disappointment.

The irony of the Bristol voyages was that the one economic resource they could have exploited was one that they chose not to. As early as 1497, Cabot's Bristol companions had noted the great quantities of cod that could be found off the coast. This fishery, stretching from Newfoundland to New England, was one of the richest in the world. In later centuries it became one of North America's most important natural resources. Bristol's explorers were probably the first to attempt commercial fishing there, bringing back a total of about 120 tons of salted fish from the expeditions of 1502 and 1504. But this may be all the fish brought back to Bristol at this time, given that they had no incentive to under-declare their catches. Indeed, given the terms of their Letters Patent, it would have been foolish not to declare every last fish taken, to ensure that Bristol's customs officers did not record it as taxable merchandise. Yet, following these early trials, Englishmen showed very little interest in the Newfoundland fisheries until the 1570s.

England's lack of interest in North America's fisheries did not mean that they were left undeveloped: a major European fishing industry was established during the sixteenth century. When the Englishman, John Rut, visited Newfoundland in 1527, he reported seeing fourteen fishing vessels just in the harbour of St Johns. But they were all French, Breton, or Portuguese.[1] By the mid-sixteenth century, hundreds of ships were taking part in the Newfoundland fishery each year, with the French expanding their operations to include further exploration, notably by Jacques Cartier, along with early attempts at settlement and trade. So, the Bristol enterprises of the period 1496-1508 did lead to the rise of a major industry and further exploration. It was just that, for most of the century, it was other European nations that benefitted.[2]

In the last decades of the sixteenth century, England began to expand its maritime horizons once more. Many argued that the country needed to develop its own overseas trade and colonies. In part this was driven by the fear that Protestant England would be crushed by the ascendant Catholic empires of Spain and Portugal; countries that had become rich from extra-European trade and the colonisation of the Americas. In response, English explorers and buccaneers, such as Sir Francis Drake and Sir Walter Raleigh, attacked Iberia's commerce and sought to establish new trade routes and colonies in the Americas. Such ambitions were now easier to achieve because rapid population growth from the 1520s had driven up the price of land and food in England. This made the establishment of foreign colonies and fisheries more appealing. Moreover, when war broke out between England and the combined powers of Spain and Portugal in 1585, the English started attacking Iberian shipping wherever they could find it. That included the

Spanish and Portuguese fishing fleets off Newfoundland. Over the next twenty years of war, English privateers drove the Iberians out. They were replaced by West Country fishermen, predominantly from Devon and Dorset, who subsequently became the dominant players in the region.[3]

Plate 57 |An eighteenth century fishing station showing the processes involved in drying cod and extracting liver oil (*John Carter Brown Library*)[4]

All this, of course, happened more than two generations after the exploration voyages discussed in this book. But the late Elizabethan endeavours had another impact: they changed the way the earlier Bristol voyages were remembered. Writers such as Richard Hakluyt and Samuel Purchas wanted to persuade people that England's destiny lay with the sea. One way of doing this was to tell people about their country's past maritime achievements. To these writers, Cabot was no longer the man who had failed to discover a route to the Orient; he was the pioneering explorer who had discovered North America and claimed it for England.[5] And North America was now seen as useful, not just for its fishery, but as land ripe for colonisation. Since Cabot had claimed this land for England in 1497, imperialists argued that England had a right to the continent by virtue of first discovery. Such claims would be advanced throughout the colonial period and, indeed, even today, the 'doctrine of discovery' underpins the historic land claims of the USA and Canada.[6]

In the late-sixteenth century Cabot became a 'hero' figure for those who wanted England to become an imperial power. As the settlement of British North America grew in the seventeenth and eighteenth century and Britain became the world's leading maritime power, the explorer's reputation also grew, even if most writers believed that the Bristol voyages were led by Sebastian Cabot, rather than his father, John. It is for these reasons that the Cabots are remembered today. Contemporaries may not have known or cared much about the exploration voyages from Bristol, but the explorers' part in the creation of English-speaking America, and the role the voyages played in the development of the British Empire, led to the expeditions being celebrated, particularly in England and Canada.[7] As a result, you cannot go far in Bristol or Newfoundland today without coming across memorials of the Cabot voyages: be that in the form of statues, paintings, buildings, street names, businesses, memorial towers and even working replicas of Cabot's ship, the *Matthew*.

Plate 58 |Cabot Memorial Tower of 1897 on Signal Hill, St John's, Newfoundland (*Photo: Shutterstock*)

Endnotes

INTRODUCTION

1. The rhyme is usually attributed to Winifred Sackville Stoner (1902-83) and a poem she published in 1919.
2. The first recorded Spanish expedition to North America was that of Juan Ponce de León in 1513, which explored the coast of Florida.

1 BRISTOL IN THE AGE OF DISCOVERY

1. Illustration from J. F. Nicholls, *Bristol Past and Present* (3 vols, Bristol, 1881-2) iii, 274.
2. For a useful summary, including references to recent scholarship, Wendy R. Childs, *Trade and Shipping in the Medieval West: Portugal, Castile and England* (Porto, 2013).
3. The best general description of Bristol's trade at this time remains: E. M. Carus-Wilson, 'The overseas trade of Bristol' in E. Power and M. M. Postan (eds.), *Studies in English Trade in the Fifteenth Century* (London, 1933).
4. Evan T. Jones, 'The shipping industry of the Severn Seas' in Evan T. Jones and Richard Stone (eds.), *The World of the Newport Ship* (University of Wales Press, forthcoming); details of individual voyages and cargoes taken from the customs accounts, including those in E. M. Carus-Wilson (ed.), *The Overseas Trade of Bristol in the later Middle Ages* (Second edn, London, 1967), passim.
5. Childs, *Trade and Shipping*, 119-122; Hilario Casado Alonso and Flavío Miranda, 'The Iberian economy and commercial exchange with north-western Europe in the later Middle Ages', in Jones and Stone, *The World of the Newport Ship*. The knowledge Bristol merchants had acquired of Portugal's Atlantic ventures seems to be reflected in William Worcestre's account of Madeira and other Atlantic islands off the coast of Africa, following his visits to Bristol in the 1480s: R. A. Skelton, 'English knowledge of the Portuguese discoveries in the 15th century: a new document', *Actas Congreso Internacional de História dos Descobrimentos*, ii (Lisbon, 1961), 367-71.
6. E. M. Carus-Wilson, 'The Iceland trade', in Power and Postan, *Studies in English Trade*, 155-71.

2 BRISTOL AND ATLANTIC EXPLORATION: THE SEARCH FOR THE ISLAND OF BRASIL

1. Claudius Ptolomaeus, *Cosmographia*, (transl.) Jacobus Angelus, (ed.) Nicolaus Germanus (Ulm, 1482). The maps were printed from woodcuts and hand coloured, so that there are numerous variations in surviving copies as well as in later facsimiles.
2. T. J. Westropp, 'Brasil and the legendary islands of the North Atlantic: their history and fable. A contribution to the "Atlantis" problem', *Proceedings of the Royal Irish Academy*, Vol XXX, Section C (1912), 223-60.
3. Permission to use this image was granted by the Italian Ministry of Heritage, Cultural Activities and Tourism on the condition that further reproduction is forbidden.
4. The exact location of Brasil on charts did naturally vary, given that nobody had actually visited it. Indeed, four of the five late-fifteenth century maps preserved in the Florentine state archives place the Island of Brasil in two places: off the coast of Ireland and off Cape St Vincent in Portugal: Archivio di Stato, Firenze, CN5-9: see Richard L. Pflederer, *Catalogue of the Portolan Charts and Atlases in the Archivio di Stato di Firenze* (Privately printed, USA, 2013). The most recent study of 'Hy-Brasil' is Barbara Freitag, *Hy-Brasil: the Metamorphosis of an Island: from Cartographic Error to Celtic Elysium* (Amsterdam, 2013), especially 3-30 and the list of maps at 265-97. Freitag's discussion includes, not just the 'Brasil' near Ireland, but also the 'Brasil' island in the region of the Azores, which is probably Terceira and perhaps named for the dye-stuff orchil; and the northern 'isle of Brasil', which first appears on the so-called Catalan map of c. 1480 and moves between 47° and 63° north until it disappeared from maps at the end of the sixteenth century.
5. Harvey L. Sharrer, 'The passing of King Arthur to the Island of Brasil in a fifteenth-century Spanish version of the post-vulgate Roman du Graal', *Romania*,

92 (1971), 65-74. The authors thank Professor Sharrer for providing them with a translation of the Spanish text.

6. In its unadulterated form, brasil produces a red dye, albeit one that was not lightfast over time; its colour could be further enhanced or altered when used in combination with other dyes: Dominique Cardon, *Natural Dyes: Sources, Tradition, Technology and Science*, (transl.) Caroline Higgitt (London, 2007), 274-88.

7. Melchior Fokkens, *Beschrijvinge der wiidjt-vermaade Koop-stadt Amstelredam* (Doornick, 1664), 716-7. The task is being performed by prison labour.

8. Wendy R. Childs, *Anglo-Castilian Trade in the Later Middle Ages* (Manchester, 1978).

9. Childs, *Trade and Shipping*, 92-4, 132-4.

10. Frances Neale (ed.), *William Worcestre: The Topography of Medieval Bristol*, (Vol. 51, Bristol Record Society, 2000), 234-35.

11. Carus-Wilson, *Overseas Trade*, 161-5; D. B. Quinn, *England and the Discovery of America 1481-1620* (London, 1974), 8-9, 73-5. For more on Croft, see C. S. L. Davies, 'Thomas Croft (c. 1436-1488), *Oxford Dictionary of National Biography* (OUP, 2004, online edn. 2008).

12. David Beers Quinn, 'The argument for the English discovery of America between 1480 and 1494', *The Geographical Journal*, Vol. 127 (1961), 277-85.

13. T. F. Reddaway and A. A. Ruddock (eds.), 'The accounts of John Balsall, purser of the *Trinity* of Bristol, 1480-1' Camden Miscellany XXIII (London, 1969), 3, 10, 24. For the size of the two *Georges* Carus-Wilson, *Overseas Trade*, 277-9, 285 from The National Archives [TNA: PRO] E122/19/14; Neale, *William Worcestre*, 140-1. Worcestre appears to suggest that the smaller *George* was the ship involved in the 'search for islands' in 1480.

14. Sixteenth-century records indicate that fishing vessels sailing to Iceland expected to use a wey of salt (40 bushels, or just over a ton) to preserve 800-1000 codfish. That works out at around 2 pints of salt per fish: E. T. Jones, 'England's Icelandic fishery in the early modern period' in D. J. Starkey et al. (eds.), *England's Sea Fisheries: The Commercial Sea Fisheries of England and Wales since 1300* (Chatham Press, 2000), 109.

15. Carol Belanger Grafton, *Medieval Life Illustrations* (1996) (reproductions of medieval woodcuts).

16. Luis A. Robles Macías, 'Revised transcription of Pedro de Ayala's 1498 report about English voyages of exploration', 11-13: www.academia.edu/12319069/. This is a translated and slightly abridged version of the article by the same author entitled 'Transcripción revisada del informe de Pedro de Ayala de 1498 sobre las expediciones inglesas de descubrimiento', *Revista de Indias*, 74, no. 262 (2014), 623-60. While Ayala's comments suggest further voyages, it would be unwise to put too much faith in the numbers or chronology quoted, since Ayala had been largely resident in Scotland until late in 1496.

17. New translation from the original manuscript by Dr. Fernando Cervantes and Gonzalo Velasco Berenguer on behalf of the authors. The first published transcript and translation of the letter by its discoverer, Louis-André Vigneras, was imperfect, as Vigneras later recognised. It is, however, still the mostly widely used translation, not least because it was included without alteration by James Williamson in his source book, James A. Williamson, *The Cabot Voyages and Bristol Discovery under Henry VII* (Hakluyt Society, 2nd Series, no. 120 (1962)), 211-4. The best published transcript of the original Spanish is that of Juan Fernández Gil and Consuela Varela, *Cartas particulares á Colón y relaciones coetáneas* (Madrid, 1984), 266-9.

18. Williamson, *Cabot Voyages*, 210.

19. Quinn, 'The argument for the English discovery of America', 277-85. A number of popular historians have propagated this notion, in great part because it implies that Bristol men reached North America before Columbus. See, for instance: Ian Wilson, *The Columbus Myth: Did Men of Bristol Reach America before Columbus?* (1992); Rodney Broome, *Amerike: The Briton who gave America its Name* (Stroud, 2002).

20. Susan Flavin and Evan T. Jones (eds.), *Bristol's Trade with Ireland and the Continent 1503-1601* (Bristol Record Society, 2009), 21, 81.

21. Cardon, *Natural Dyes*, 275, 279-81, 285-9.

3 JOHN CABOT: BACKGROUND

1. Robles Macías, 'Revised transcription of Pedro de Ayala's 1498 report'.
2. Williamson, *Cabot Voyages*, 190-91.
3. E. Giuffrida, 'New documents on Giovanni Caboto', in R. Mamoli Zorzi (ed.) *Attraversare gli Oceani: Da Giovanni Caboto al Canada Multiculturale* (Venice, 1999), 62, 64-5. Giuffrida is the discoverer of the only known examples of Cabot's signature.
4. Although now known as Cabot's house, the memorial plaque affixed to the house in 1881 claims only that he lived in the Castello area of the city, in which this house is situated.
5. The Mamluk sultanate extended from Egypt through lands known in medieval times as the Levant, which included the important ports of Beirut and Tripoli, and stretched through modern Israel and Syria. The sultanate included also the Hejaz on the east side of the Red Sea, as far south as Mecca. For Cabot's purchase of a slave in one of the trading posts of the Sultanate, Giuffrida, 'New documents on Giovanni Caboto', 63.
6. Giuffrida, 'New documents on Giovanni Caboto', 47–71.
7. M. F. Tiepolo, 'Documenti Veneziani su Giovanni Caboto', *Studi Veneziani*, xv (1973), 585–97.
8. M. Ballesteros-Gaibrois, 'Juan Caboto en España: nueva luz sobre un problema viejo', *Revista de Indias*, iv (1943), 607–27; supporting documents translated in Williamson, *Cabot Voyages*, 196-9.
9. Juan Gil, *Mitos y utopías del Descubrimiento: I. Colón y su tiempo* (Madrid, 1989), 77-81; partial translation into English of the documents in Francisco Albardaner i Llorens, 'John Cabot and Christopher Columbus revisited', *The Northern Mariner*, 10 no 2 (2000), 93-4.
10. It has been suggested that Cabot might have accompanied Columbus' 1493 expedition, returning to Spain the following year: Douglas Hunter, *Race to the New World: Christopher Columbus, John Cabot, and a Lost History of Discovery* (Palgrave Macmillan, 2011), 78-82, 91-3. While possible on grounds of chronology, there is no firm evidence for this, and no crew list for Columbus' 1493 expedition has yet been found.
11. Robles Macías, 'Revised transcription of Pedro de Ayala's 1498 report'.
12. 1492/3: Total value of trade £33,890, Andalusia £4984 (15%), Portugal £7,674 (23%). Calculated from the Bristol customs ledger for September 1492-3, TNA: PRO, E122/20/9.
13. M. Bratchel, 'Italian merchant organisation and business relationships in early Tudor London', *The Journal of European Economic History*, 7 (1978), 5-31; Giuliano Pinto, 'Cultura mercantile ed espansione economica di Firenze (secoli XIII-XVI)' in G. Pinto et al. (eds.), *Vespucci, Firenze e le Americhe* (Florence, 2014), 3-18. Studies in English of individual banks are few, but Raymond de Roover, *The Rise and Decline of the Medici Bank 1397-1494* (London, 1963) is a classic.
14. The support given by Giannotto Berardi to Columbus is well known and documented. But, for example, Bartolomeo Marchionni, resident in Lisbon, was an investor in the voyage of Cabral that 'found' Brasil; he continued as a significant investor and trader in the Portuguese trading fleets to India. In 1523 at least thirteen Florentines invested in a voyage under the French flag of Giovanni da Verazzano: Francesco Guidi Bruscoli, *Bartolomeo Marchionni 'Homem de grossa fazenda' (ca. 1450-1530): Un mercanto fiorentino a Lisbona e l'impero Portoghese* (Florence, 2014), esp. 140-75. For these and other examples of Florentine finance, Francesco Guidi Bruscoli, 'Capitali fiorentini nei prima viaggi verso il Nord America: Giovanni Caboto e Giovanni da Verrazano', in Pinto, *Vespucci, Firenze e le Americhe*, 105-121; and C. Verlinden, 'La Colonie Italienne de Lisbonne et le developpement de l'economie metropolitaine et colonial Portugaise' in *Studi in onore di Armando Sapori* (2 vols, Milan, 1957), I, 617-28.

4 CABOT'S PLAN: LONDON AND BRISTOL

1. Williamson, *Cabot Voyages*, 204-5. The 'letters patent' was a solemn legal document that Cabot could show openly and which carried the King's great seal.
2. Williamson, *Cabot Voyages*, 209-11. Soncino had been in England only a few months.

He crossed the Channel 23 August 1497, too late to witness Cabot's return, but had been in touch with his fellow countrymen before then.

3. Bronze medal formerly attributed to Caradosso Foppa. The reverse shows Sforza on his throne and the fortified harbor of Genoa (V&A, 7664-1861).

4. E. T. Jones, 'The *Matthew* of Bristol and the financiers of John Cabot's 1497 voyage to North America', *English Historical Review*, 121 (2006), 778-95.

5. E. T. Jones, 'Alwyn Ruddock: "John Cabot and the Discovery of America"', *Historical Research*, 81, (May, 2008), 224-254; Cal. State Papers Milan, I, 321-3; Williamson, *Cabot Voyages*, 227.

6. Charles Knight, *Old England: A Pictorial Museum* (2 vols, London, c.1860), i, 345. For the suggestion that Cabot lodged in the London Austin Friars, based on a seventeenth-century reference, Jones, 'Alwyn Ruddock', 231-2.

7. Jones, 'Alwyn Ruddock', 228; this is now known to be a minimum number, excluding at least one of her most important finds. See also Evan T. Jones, 'Bristol, Cabot and the New Found Land, 1496-1500' in P. E. Pope and S. Lewis-Simpson (eds.) *Exploring Atlantic Transitions: Archaeologies of Permanence and Transience in New Found Lands* (Woodbridge, 2013), 27-30.

8. Francesco Guidi Bruscoli, 'John Cabot and his Italian Financiers', *Historical Research*, 85 (August, 2012), 372-93.

9. Williamson, *Cabot Voyages*, 207-11.

10. Williamson, *Cabot Voyages*, 210.

11. Although no detailed customs accounts survive from the period of the Iceland trade's height (c.1430-50), later accounts reveal that the value of the goods carried by merchantmen sailing to or from Iceland was relatively small. For instance, when the *Anthony* of Bristol, left for Iceland in 1466, its exports were valued at £106, which amounts to about 1% of the total recorded exports (£12,932) that took place between 29 Sept 1465 and 14 May 1466. Similarly, when the 'navis' (great ship) the *Trinity* of London, returned from Iceland on 18 Sept 1486, the declared value of its goods was £238. This represents 2% of imports (£13,607) that year. This suggests that, even when the Iceland venture trade was at its height, with perhaps three or four great ships sailing north each year, it would still have represented a very minor component of Bristol's overall trade.

12. TNA: PRO, E122/20/5, fo. 31r; E122/20/7; E122/20/9, fo. 41v; licence to named Bristol merchants for two ships 1488-9, TNA: PRO, C76/173, m. 15. The London owner of the 1486 *Trinity* seems subsequently to have transferred his interest to the east coast route.

13. E. M. Carus-Wilson, 'The Iceland Trade', 182; Quinn, *Discovery of America*, 47-50.

14. W. R. Childs, 'England's Icelandic trade in the fifteenth century: The role of the port of Hull', *Northern Seas* (1995), 11-31.

15. Jones, 'England's Icelandic fishery in the early modern period', 106-7.

16. Richard Stone, 'Bristol's overseas trade in the later fifteenth century', in Jones and Stone, *World of the Newport Ship*.

17. TNA: PRO, E122/20/9.

5 1496 AND 1497 EXPEDITIONS

1. Translated from the Spanish of the original manuscript by Dr. Fernando Cervantes and Gonzalo Velasco Berenguer on behalf of the authors.

2. G. E. Weare, *Cabot's Discovery of North America* (London, 1897), 116.

3. Williamson, *Cabot Voyages*, 207-14.

4. For the Burgundian and the Genoese, see Soncino's letter, Williamson, *Cabot Voyages*, 211. David Quinn and others have suggested that the 'Burgundian' could have been the globe-maker and adventurer Martin Behaim: but in the current state of knowledge it is unlikely that this man's identity will ever be known with certainty.

5. On crew ratios in the latter half of the fifteenth century, see Childs, *Trade and Shipping*, 86; Ian Friel, 'The rise and fall of the Big Ship, 1400-1520' in Jones and Stone, *World of the Newport Ship*.

6. TNA: PRO, E101/414/16, fo. 12r and below, Chapter 7.

7. The statue of John Cabot is by Hans Mills (1970).

8. Williamson, *Cabot Voyages*, 208-9, 212.

9. J. P. Howley, *The Mineral Resources of Newfoundland* (St. John's, Newfoundland, 1892), 35-6; Ingeborg Marshall, *A History and Ethnography of the Beothuk*, (Montreal, 1996), esp. 14-16, 337-41, 387-420, 441; William Gilbert, 'Beothuk-European contact in the 16th century: a re-evaluation of the documentary evidence', *Acadiensis*, XXXX, no.1 (2011), 24-44. For Beothuk tools and hunting methods, albeit from sparse evidence, see Marshall, *History and Ethnography*, 311-6, 327-33.

10. Williamson, *Cabot Voyages*, 214; M. M. Condon, 'Itinerary of Henry VII' (unpublished) under date.

11. 'Remains of Henry the 2nd's Palace as it stood in Woodstock park in 1714': published for Samuel Ireland (1744-1800) in 1799. The surviving buildings were demolished in 1723. In the fifteenth century Woodstock was always known as a 'manor' rather than a 'palace'.

12. Williamson, *Cabot Voyages*, 207-8.

13. The best account of the rebellion is Ian Arthurson, *The Perkin Warbeck Conspiracy 1491-1499* (Stroud, 1994), 169-201.

14. *Cal. State Papers Milan*, I, no. 545.

15. Jones, 'Bristol, Cabot and the New Found Land', 29. As in other instances of casual payments to Cabot, the explorer is identified by description, and not by name. In this instance he is described as 'a lumbard [a general word for Italians] that found thisle'.

16. Condon, 'Itinerary'.

17. Payment at the King's 'pleasure' meant this was a conditional grant rather than a grant for life, although the two were often synonymous. It would be a further six weeks before the grant of 13 December was given effective legal validity by the issue of letters patent under the King's great seal. This delay may have taken place, in part, simply because Cabot would have had to pay the considerable costs involved in having the formal patent drawn up: Margaret M. Condon and Evan T. Jones (eds.), 'The grant of a pension of £20 per year to John Cabot, 13 December 1497' (University of Bristol, ROSE, 2011): http://hdl.handle.net/1983/1792.

6   THE MYSTERY OF THE 1498 VOYAGE

1. Williamson, *Cabot Voyages*, 209-11.

2. Williamson, *Cabot Voyages*, 226-7. The initiative for seeking the patent came from Cabot, who petitioned the King directly. He is likely, however, to have acted on advice and may well have received official encouragement for doing so.

3. The Great Chronicle of London is one of the major narrative accounts for the period and was completed in its present form around 1512, albeit much would have been copied from earlier records. For the date, possible authorship, and sources for the Great Chronicle: A. H. Thomas and I. D. Thornley (eds.), *The Great Chronicle of London* (London, 1938); Mary-Rose McClaren, *The London Chronicles of the Fifteenth Century* (Woodbridge, 2002).

4. Williamson, *Cabot Voyages*, 220-21.

5. Williamson, *Cabot Voyages*, 214-15.

6. Jones, 'Alwyn Ruddock', 242-3.

7. Williamson, *Cabot Voyages*, 215.

8. Williamson, *Cabot Voyages*, 103-11, 220-23. Annotations in the original manuscript of the Great Chronicle are a year out when translating regnal years into years AD.

9. Williamson, *Cabot Voyages*, pp. 224-5; Denys Hay, 'The manuscript of Polydore Vergil's "Anglica Historia"', *English Historical Review*, 54 (1939), pp. 246-7.

10. Discussed in Williamson, *Cabot Voyages*, 72-83, 107-9, 298-307. The original is in the Museo Naval, Madrid. Scholarly literature on the La Cosa map is extensive and frequently contradictory. It includes a major monograph by Fernando Silío Cervera (1995). A recent contribution, by Luis Robles Macías (2010), using new methodology, suggests that, for the Americas, latitudes are very nearly accurate from south-east Cuba to the Amazon, but show increasing distortion and cartographic invention to both north and south as the mapmaker attempted to make sense of a jigsaw of information fragments from recent expeditions, including those of John Cabot.

11. Lucas Janszoon Waghenaear, (ed. and transl. Anthony Ashley), *The Mariners Mirrour* (London, 1588).

12. Robles Macías, 'Revised transcription of Pedro de Ayala's 1498 report', 13.

13. Williamson, *Cabot Voyages*, 109-10, 233-4.
14. The early nineteenth century historian Martín Fernández de Navarrete was convinced that the 1498 expedition had reached the region of Coquibaçoa on the north-east coast of Venezuela, but no firm evidence to support his assertion has ever been found. James Williamson pointed to a short section of the Venezuelan coast in La Cosa's map which appeared to be accurate beyond the point known to have been reached by Spanish expeditions by 1500: but, in a judgment with which the authors concur, was reluctant to draw firm conclusions from it: Williamson, *Cabot Voyages*, 108-12.
15. Jones, 'Alwyn Ruddock', 244-9; see also Williamson, *Cabot Voyages*, 93. Today Carbonear is a town of c.5,000 people. Recent archaeological investigations by Professor Peter Pope (Memorial University, Newfoundland), revealed traces of seventeenth-nineteenth century settlement in the area but found no evidence of earlier European habitation.
16. Jones, 'Bristol, Cabot and the New Found Land', 28-30.
17. Ruddock believed that Giovanni Antonio did not come back: Jones, 'Alwyn Ruddock', 249. There is no mention of Carbonariis in Milanese correspondence with England in 1499; and the record then ceases entirely until 1513, following the capture by the French of both the city and its duke.

7   BRISTOL AND THE 'NEW FOUND LAND': 1499-1508 VOYAGES

1. Evan T. Jones, 'Henry VII and the Bristol expeditions to North America: the Condon documents', *Historical Research*, 83 (August, 2010), 444-54. For a more detailed and updated discussion of the letter, see: Margaret M. Condon and Evan T. Jones (eds.), 'Henry VII's letter to John Morton concerning William Weston's voyage to the new found land' (University of Bristol, ROSE, 2011): http://hdl.handle.net/1983/1734.
2. Jones and Condon, 'William Weston: early explorer of the New World', forthcoming.
3. For the first use of these words, see: *Oxford English Dictionary*.
4. On 4 May 1493 Pope Alexander VI had issued the papal bull *Inter Caetera*, which specified that all newly discovered lands that lay west of a meridian lying 100 leagues west of the Azores would belong to Spain. All lands to the east of the meridian would belong to Portugal. While this line of demarcation was modified by the Treaty of Tordesillas, the papal bull, in effect, meant the Pope was sanctioning a division of the non-Christian – and still largely unknown – world into two hemispheres, one of which was to 'belong' to Spain and the other to Portugal.
5. Robles Macías, 'Revised transcription of Pedro de Ayala's 1498 report'.
6. The arms appear also on several important metal objects recently recovered from a wreck from Vasco da Gama's second Indian fleet of 1502-3: David L. Mearns et al, 'A Portuguese East-Indiaman from the 1502-1503 Fleet of Vasco da Gama off Hallaniyah Island, Oman: an interim Report', *International Journal of Nautical History* (2016), 14-17.
7. For Pedro Reinel's map (Kunstmann I) Williamson, *Cabot Voyages*, 316; Maria Fernanda Alegria et al., 'Portuguese Cartography in the Renaissance' in David Woodward (ed.), *The History of Cartography*, Vol 3 pt i (Chicago, 2007), 986.
8. Williamson, *Cabot Voyages*, 118-24, 229-30, 312-9 and Plates IV, XII, and XIII (Cantino, Reinel, and Kunstmann III); H. P. Biggar, *The Precursors of Jaques Cartier* (Ottawa, 1911), 61-7; Alegria, 'Portuguese Cartography', 986, 992-4. Juan de la Cosa's 1500 manuscript map, which *does* appear to preserve some 'Cabot' names, was the work of a Spanish cartographer at a time when the Portuguese were making major discoveries: and was not used by later mapmakers. Alberto Cantino, an Italian diplomat based in Lisbon, commissioned, on behalf of the Duke of Ferrara, the 1502 map that now bears his name. The map incorporates the latest discovery information, even though the explorers' charts were closely guarded state secrets.
9. Williamson, *Cabot Voyages*, 241, 255.
10. The Azoreans were also offered naturalisation. This would have given them legal rights and some of the fiscal advantages of native-born Englishmen, but would have required them to swear allegiance to Henry VII as their overlord. This seems not to have happened.

11. Biggar, *Precursors*, 7-8, 41-50; Williamson, *Cabot Voyages*, 235-47.

12. This voyage probably took place under the terms of the 1501 patent, although it might have taken place under Cabot's earlier patent, which was still valid.

13. Williamson, *Cabot Voyages*, 215, 247-8; TNA: PRO, E101/415/3, fo. 79v. A tally was a notched wooden stick representing a sum of money: and is best thought of as a primitive form of cheque, with built-in safeguards against forgery. The *Gabriel* was expected to enter Bristol from Bordeaux, at which point the merchants would claim their exemption from customs dues.

14. For the Thorne letter, Williamson, *Cabot Voyages*, 26-9, 202, and A. A. Ruddock, 'The Reputation of Sebastian Cabot', *Bulletin of the Institute of Historical Research*, xlii (1974), 96. The full text is in D. B. Quinn, *New American World: a Documentary History of North America to 1612* (5 vols, London, 1979), I, 182-9.

15. Condon, 'Itinerary'.

16. Williamson, *Cabot Voyages*, 248-49.

17. Williamson, *Cabot Voyages*, 220. Spelling modernised with comments added in roman; see also Gilbert, 'Beothuk-European contact', 28-9.

18. Williamson, *Cabot Voyages*, 309-22; see also the letter of Robert Thorne the younger to Dr. Edward Lee in 1527, in Quinn, *New American World*, I, 184, 187-8.

19. Williamson, *Cabot Voyages*, 216 from TNA: PRO, E101/415/3, fos. 103r, v.

20. Ruddock, 'Reputation of Sebastian Cabot', 98; Quinn, *New American World*, I, 110. The size of a 'last' varied depending on the commodity but in this case the record makes clear that the calculation had been based on three tons to the last.

21. A. E. Nordenskiöld, *Periplus: an Essay on the early history of Charts and Sailing Directions* (Stockholm, 1897).

22. With this new grant, João Fernandes, Richard Warde, and John Thomas, the other patent holders of 1501, were specifically excluded from further participation unless by licence of Eliot and his fellow patentees, and would be required to pay their share of costs.

23. Williamson, *Cabot Voyages*, 250-61. Latin text in Biggar, *Precursors*, 70-81.

24. Williamson, *Cabot Voyages*, 216. Since Williamson wrote, the original chamber book has become available, British Library Add. MS 59899, fos. 32v, 38r. For the King's movements, Condon, 'Itinerary'. The weapons were brought to the king by a servant of Sir Walter Herbert; the giver of the hawks is unknown.

25. Williamson, *Cabot Voyages*, p. 137-8; Ruddock, 'Reputation of Sebastian Cabot', 95-9.

26. Jones, '*Matthew* of Bristol', 785.

27. The new charter of 1499 required two sheriffs, serving jointly.

28. At this date, ships rarely carried a priest to say mass or minister to the crew, and the presumption must be that his intention was to be land-based; for the 'dry mass' and religious observance on board ship, Vincent V. Patarino jnr., 'The Religious Culture of Sixteenth- and Seventeenth-Century English Sailors', in Cheryl Fury (ed.), *The Social History of English Seamen 1485-1649* (Woodbridge, 2012), 149-55.

29. Williamson, *Cabot Voyages*, 216; BL Add MS 59899, fo. 53r.

30. Ruddock, 'Reputation of Sebastian Cabot', 97-8.

31. Jones, 'Henry VII and the Bristol expeditions to North America', 452-3. The reward was made within two years of Michaelmas (29 September) 1502.

32. BL Add MS 59899, fo. 96v, correcting date in Williamson, *Cabot Voyages*, 216.

33. Williamson, *Cabot Voyages*, 263-4.

34. A. P. Newton, 'An early grant to Sebastian Cabot' *English Historical Review*, Vol. 37 (1922), 564-5, corrected by Ruddock, 'The reputation of Sebastian Cabot', 96-9.

35. D. B. Quinn, *Sebastian Cabot and Bristol Exploration* (Local history pamphlets, Bristol Branch of the Historical Association, 1968).

36. Samuel Seyer, *Memorials Historical and Topographical of Bristol and its Neighbourhood* (2 vols, Bristol, 1821-3), ii, plate between 208-9.

37. Henry Harrisse, *John Cabot, the Discoverer of North-America and Sebastian, his Son: A Chapter of the Maritime History of England under the Tudors, 1496-1557* (London, 1896); Peter Pope, *The Many Landfalls of John Cabot* (Toronto, 1997), 43-68.

38. Quinn, *New American World*, I, 121-3, including a translation of Cabot's receipt. In May 1509 Cabot was also paid both installments for 1507. This could suggest the

voyage was actually 1507/8, or that it was of longer duration than is generally supposed.

39. Williamson, *Cabot Voyages*, 266-9; see also Ruddock, 'Reputation of Sebastian Cabot', 95-6.

40. Williamson, *Cabot Voyages*, 165-6.

41. Williamson, *Cabot Voyages*, 270.

42. J. A. Williamson, *The Voyages of the Cabots and the English Discovery of North America under Henry VII and Henry VIII* (London, 1929), 244-71.

8 THE NAMING OF THE LAND

1. Williamson, *Cabot Voyages*, 214-6; British Library, Add. MS 59899, fo. 38r; Condon and Jones, 'Henry VII's letter to John Morton'.

2. Felipe Fernández-Armesto, *Amerigo, the man who gave his name to America* (London, 2006), 146-50, 183-203; Alfred Hiatt, *Terra Incognita: Mapping the Antipodes before 1600* (London, 2008), pp. 191-8.

3. Translation and photograph of Latin original in John W. Hessler, *The Naming of America: Martin Waldseemuller's 1507 World Map and the Cosmographiae Introductio* (London, 2008), 52, 101.

4. Waldseemüller also produced printed globe gores that could be cut out and pasted on to a sphere to create a globe. These have a simplified version of the map but still label the southern continent as America: illustration, Hessler, *Naming of America*, 36-9. Five sets of the gores, including a later variant, have now been found. The most recent discovery is University Library of Munich, ULM Cim. 107#2, with the name 'America' prominent on the southern continent. Made up, the globes would have been very small – little more than four and a half inches in diameter.

5. Hessler, *Naming of America*, 18, 24-5, including illustrations.

6. Hessler, *Naming of America*, 12-13, 16-17, including illustrations. Cabot and the Corte Reals are not mentioned. The land Gaspar Corte Real explored is labelled as an unknown shore, and floats in the sea beneath the portrait of Ptolemy. It is barely legible in the small-scale reproduction in Hessler, but can be identified by the Portuguese flag.

7. Hessler, *Naming of America*, 46; more fully in John W. Hessler and Chet van Duzer, *Seeing the World Anew: the radical vision of Martin Waldseemüller's 1507 & 1516 world maps* (Florida, 2012), 19-22. Only a single copy (discovered in 1901) survives. It was purchased by the Library of Congress in 2003 and is now referenced as G3200 1507.W3.

8. Christine R. Johnson, 'German Cosmographers and the Naming of America', *Past and Present*, 191 (2006), 3-43 explores the intellectual context of Waldseemüller and Ringmann's naming of the land, and its enduring use.

9. Williamson, *Cabot Voyages*, 202, 262-3; F. F. Fox and J. Taylor, *Some Account of the Guild of Weavers in Bristol: Chiefly from MSS* (Bristol, 1889), 92. The quote comes from a petition from Bristol's fullers of c. 1568, addressed to the town's mayor, which summarises an earlier city petition to Elizabeth I.

10. E. Scott and A. E. Hudd (eds.), *'The Cabot Roll': The customs roll of the port of Bristol* (Bristol, 1897), facsimile.

11. Hudd had been alerted to the existence of the manuscript by 'Mr Coote of the British Museum'. The document had been found by Edward Scott, the Keeper of Manuscripts at the Museum 1888-91 and from 1891 Keeper of Muniments at Westminster Abbey. Extracts in translation in Williamson, *Cabot Voyages*, 219.

12. Alfred E. Hudd, 'Richard Ameryk and the name America', *Proceedings of the Clifton Antiquarian Club*, vii (1909-10), 1-9.

13. TNA: PRO, E356/23, E122/26/13, and E326/3264. The name 'Amerike', which perhaps looks most similar to 'America', comes from his daughter's tomb brass in St Mary Redcliffe church, Bristol. She died in September 1538.

14. Suit for debt brought by William Byrd against Richard Meryk 'of Chapstow' in 1477, Bristol Record Office JTol//J/1/1, fo. 74. For the Welsh in Bristol, Peter Fleming, 'The Severn Sea: Urban Networks and Connections in the Fifteenth Century' in Jones and Stone, *World of the Newport Ship*.

15. Ap Meryk is first found shipping through Bristol in 1472. For his trade in 1475 and

1479-80, Carus-Wilson, *Overseas Trade*, 203-4 [1475]; 246, 256, 263, 268, 278, 280 [1479-80].

16. *Cal. Fine Rolls* 1485-1509, pp. 51-2; TNA: PRO, E356/24, rot. 1.

17. Bristol Record Office, (BRO) 04720, fo. 134v; Addams Chronicle, BRO, 13748/4 under date, confirmed by TNA: PRO, E372/349 Bristol.

18. *Cal. Fine Rolls* 1485-1509, pp. 199-200; *Cal. Patent Rolls* 1485-1494, 269. Kemys and the previous customer, John Walshe, in effect swapped offices, with Walshe replacing Kemys as controller.

19. *Cal. Patent Rolls*, 1494-1509, 43, 171; TNA: PRO, E101/414/16, fo. 134v. Ap Meryk is to be the subject of a future article by Condon and Jones.

20. W. St. Clair Baddeley, 'A Bristol rental, 1498-9', *Transactions of the Bristol and Gloucestershire Archaeological Society*, no. 47 (1925), 126 (original roll now Gloucestershire Archives, MS D674/a/Z9).

21. By 1490 Arthur Kemys had placed his nephew, John, in the household of Philip Grene, a Bristol grocer, transferring (for a sum of money) the custody known as wardship. Grene, as was not unusual, married his daughter to his ward *Cal. Patent Rolls*, 1485-94, 86; Bristol RO 5139/167; TNA: PRO, PROB11/14, fo. 64r.

22. For an example of the latter, Carus-Wilson, *Overseas Trade*, 150-1.

23. For more on this, see: Margaret M. Condon and Evan T. Jones, 'Warrant for the payment of John Cabot's Pension, 22 February 1498' (University of Bristol, PURE, 2011): http://hdl.handle.net/1983/1795.

24. That 'America' first appears as the name for the southern continent, which John Cabot did not explore, and was not used for the northern one for at least sixty years, has been ignored by advocates of the 'Amerike' theory.

9   SHIPS AND SAILORS OF THE DISCOVERY VOYAGES

1. Weare, *Cabot's Discovery of North America*, 116 quoting from a copy of a Bristol chronicle written in 1565.

2. The 1503/4 ledger is the first full-year account to survive since that for 1492/3. The accounting year started at Michaelmas (29 September). Modern edition in Flavin and Jones, *Bristol's Trade with Ireland and the Continent*, 1-102.

3. Jones, '*Matthew* of Bristol', 786. The spellings of the ships have been modernised here. The figures in brackets are tonnages recorded in sources other than the account: ibid., 785 nn. 23-4.

4. M. M. Condon and Evan T. Jones, 'New light on the *Matthew* of Bristol' (forthcoming).

5. Jones, 'The *Matthew* of Bristol', 785.

6. Condon and Jones, 'New light on the *Matthew*'.

7. A well-known collection of Bristol merchant marks over several centuries, drawn from Bristol sources, is Alfred E. Hudd, *Bristol Merchants Marks* (Bristol, 1912).

8. Childs, *Trade and Shipping*, p. 86; Friel, 'Rise and fall of the Big Ship'.

9. Louis- André Vigneras, 'The Three Brothers Guerra of Triana and their Five Voyages to the New World, 1498-1504', *The Hispanic American Historical Review*, 52 (1972), 635-6. A similarly high ratio of 1:3 or 1:3.5 operated for English ships in the mid-sixteenth century Guinea trade: J. D. Alsop, 'Tudor Merchant Seafarers in the Early Guinea Trade' in Fury, *Social History of English Seamen*, 87-8. The fifty-ton *Vizcaina*, used by Columbus in 1502, similarly carried 23 men, including a chaplain: Franco Gay and Cesare Ciano, *The Ships of Christopher Columbus*, trans. L Bertolazzi and L. F. Farina (Rome, 1996), 255.

10. Reddaway and Ruddock, 'The accounts of John Balsall', 8.

11. C. Varela, *Cristóbal Colón: de corsario a Almirante* (Barcelona, 2005), 92.

12. Evidence relating to the age of mariners comes mostly from the sixteenth century: see G. V. Scammell, 'Manning the English merchant service in the sixteenth century', *Mariners Mirror*, 56 (1970), esp. 133, 136-40, 146-51; Ann Stirland, 'The men of the Mary Rose', in Fury, *Social History of English Seamen*, 47-73; Alsop, 'Tudor Merchant Seafarers', 88-92.

13. Cheryl A. Fury, 'Health and Health Care at Sea', in Fury, *Social History of English Seamen*, pp. 194-8. When Henry VII's great ship, the *Sovereign*, was moored in the Thames in the winter of 1496-7, the mariners left on board to safeguard her were

each allowed around ten pints a day: M. Oppenheim (ed.), *Naval Accounts and Inventories of the Reign of Henry VII* (Navy Records Society, viii, 1896), 163 [calculated using a tun of 240 gallons].

14. Bob Trett (ed.), *Newport Medieval Ship: A Guide* (Newport, 2011), 21; Margaret Rule, *The Mary Rose* (London, 1982), 190-1, 198-9.
15. Tolsey Court Book, Bristol Record Office 08154(1), p. 158; cited (including the verse that follows, and repeated refrain) Carus-Wilson, 'Overseas trade of Bristol' in Power and Postan, *Studies in English Trade*, 190-1.

10 AFTERMATH

1. Williamson, *Voyages of the Cabots* (1929), 104-5.
2. E. Jones, 'Bristol and Newfoundland 1490-1570', in I. Bulgin (ed.), *Cabot and his World Symposium, June 1997* (Newfoundland Historical Society, 1999), 73-81; Peter E. Pope, *Fish into Wine* (Chapel Hill, 2004), 11-32; Michael Huxley Barkham, 'La industria pesquera en el País Vasco peninsular al principio de la Edad Moderna: una edad de oro?', *Istas Memoria: Revista de Estudios Marítimos de País Vasco* (vol. 3, 2000), 54-65.
3. G. T. Cell, *English Enterprise in Newfoundland 1577-1660* (Toronto, 1969).
4. *Il Gazettiere Americano*, (publ. Marco Coltellini, Livorno, 1763), iii, 154.
5. David Armitage, *The Ideological Origins of the British Empire* (CUP, 2000), 61-99; Peter C. Mancall, *Hakluyt's Promise: an Elizabethan's Obsession for an English America* (Yale, 2007).
6. L. C. Green, 'Claims to territory in colonial America', in L. C. Green and O. P. Dickason, *The Law of Nations and the New World* (Edmonton, 1993).
7. For the Canadian reception and memorialisation of the voyages, see: Peter Pope, *The Many Landfalls of John Cabot* (Toronto, 1997).

Further Reading:

James A. Williamson, *The Cabot Voyages and Bristol Discovery under Henry VII* (Hakluyt Society, 2nd series, cxx, 1962). While dated, this remains the classic account of the Bristol voyages.

Peter Pope, *The Many Landfalls of John Cabot* (Toronto, 1997). Particularly useful for its examination of the reception and memorialisation of the voyages.

Evan T. Jones, 'Alwyn Ruddock: "John Cabot and the Discovery of America"', *Historical Research*, 81 (2008). Sets the agenda for a new history of John Cabot. This article can be downloaded for free from: http://onlinelibrary.wiley.com/doi/10.1111/ j.1468-2281.2007.00422.x/abstract

The University of Bristol's **'Cabot Project'** website includes a number of document transcriptions, many with extended introductory essays; and clickable links to several articles by Evan Jones. The page is regularly updated: http://www.bristol.ac.uk/ history/research/cabot.html

Evan Jones and Margaret Condon are currently writing a major academic monograph on the Bristol discovery voyages that incorporates their full findings. *Cabot and Bristol's Age of Discovery* is a digest of their existing work on the topic.

General discovery literature is extensive; and some of it is easily accessible, including:-

David Abulafia, *The Discovery of Mankind: Atlantic encounters in the Age of Columbus* (London, 2008). This is a very readable survey from a particular viewpoint, inclusive of contacts with indigenous peoples.

J. H. Parry, *The Age of Reconnaissance: discovery, exploration and settlement 1450-1650* (London, 1963) offers a useful overview, but is in need of updating.

Douglas Hunter, *The Race to the New World* (New York, 2011) is a modern popular history contrasting John Cabot and Christopher Columbus. It advances the theory that the German cosmographer Martin Behaim was the real inspiration behind Cabot's 1497 expedition.